Biblical Woman

BIBLICAL WOMAN

Contemporary Reflections on Scriptural Texts

Denise Lardner Carmody

CROSSROAD · NEW YORK

1988

The Crossroad Publishing Company
370 Lexington Avenue, New York, N.Y. 10017

Copyright © 1988 by Denise Lardner Carmody

Printed in the United States of America

Library of Congress Cataloging-in-Publication Data

Carmody, Denise Lardner, 1935–
Biblical woman : contemporary reflections on scriptural texts /
Denise Lardner Carmody.
p. cm.
Bibliography: p.
ISBN 0-8245-0892-0
1. Woman (Theology)-Biblical teaching. 2. Women in the Bible.
3. Feminism-Religious aspects-Christianity. I. Title.
BS680.W7C37 1988
220.8'3054-dc19   88-20421
                                                          CIP

For Susan Resneck Parr

Contents

Preface

I have been teaching courses on women and religion for nearly fifteen years. Inevitably, the biblical texts bearing on women's status and nature have evoked considerable discussion. For even when the course is on women and the world religions and the students are not fundamentalists, the heritage one finds in the Hebrew Bible and the New Testament remains a potent factor. The Bible has so strongly influenced the Western religious and cultural imagination that anyone seeking perspective on central matters such as the status of women has to confront the biblical materials. To most students' surprise, such a confrontation regularly turns out to be liberating. Individual texts often take surprising turns that show them to have originally been quite different from the dogmatic teachings associated with them by the churches and synagogues, while the entire mosaic makes it clear that the Bible as a whole is complex, many-voiced, and anything but simplistic.

For some time, therefore, I have looked forward to writing a small book that would illustrate biblical materials bearing on women's religious experience. The main audience I have in mind is the students who populate courses on women and religion like those I have taught, but I assume that various adult education groups, Jewish and Christian, might also find materials such as these provocative. My goal has been to illustrate various biblical perspectives on women by commenting on representative texts, and throughout I have been conscious of a twofold obligation. First, I have felt obliged to explain the background and context of the particular passage under consideration. Second, I have tried to suggest what the passage might mean (imply, stimulate, reveal) for present-day feminists, both female and male. The result, I hope, is a persuasive invitation to readers to join the conversation between tradition and current culture that theologians as diverse as Karl Barth and Bernard Lonergan have placed at the heart of faith's efforts to gain understanding.

My thanks to the students in my courses on women and religion and on biblical topics, who have stimulated me to meditate on texts such as those treated in this book, and to Frank Oveis, my patient editor at The Crossroad Publishing Company.

Introduction

The individual reflections that make up the bulk of this book focus on particular biblical texts. For our purposes, the main task in dealing with such particular texts is twofold: *(a)* to situate the text historically and explain how it fits into the larger literary unit of which it is a part, and *(b)* to suggest some of the present-day implications the text seems to carry. The Bible is more than the sum of its particular textual parts, however, so it will be useful from the outset to have an introductory overview of what the Bible as a whole assumes and says about women.

Representative of current scholarship on the general status of women in the Bible is Tikva S. Frymer-Kensky's article in the recently published *Harper's Bible Dictionary.*[1] Frymer-Kensky first treats the legal status of women in the period of the ancestors, the patriarchs and matriarchs we find in Genesis. Then she deals with women in what she calls classical Israel, focusing on women's domestic roles in settled Israelite society. Her third topic is the nondomestic roles women played. Fourth, she treats the images of biblical woman. Fifth, she studies what she calls the nonhuman female. Her sixth topic is New Testament views of women. Seventh and last, Frymer-Kensky describes the new approaches that feminist interests recently have sponsored. Each of these seven headings has relevance to the concerns of this book.

First, the legal status of women in the period of the ancestors (prior to the founding of the monarchy, around 1000

B.C.E. [before the common era]) is that of complete dependence. The head of the extended family is male, the family
line is traced through males, and a female moves into the
family circle of the man she marries. Prior to marriage a girl is
subject to the authority of her father. At marriage she passes
over to the dominion of the male head of the extended family
she joins. She has few rights over her own children, and if her
husband dies, she can be passed to one of her brothers-in-law.
Men can be polygamous, and women tend to exert influence
only through their husbands or by trickery. Legally, women
are property, and although they are supposed to be treated
well, such incidents as the offer of Lot's daughters to the men
of Sodom (Gen. 19:8) suggest the abuses—indeed, the ter-
rors—to which women are liable.[2]

Second, in classical Israel the basic social unit is the nuclear
family. (The royal family, which includes the king's harem, is
an exception.) Women still are under the dominion of their
husbands, but less absolutely than in the period of the ancestors. Sons rank lower than mothers, and children owe
obedience to their mothers as well as their fathers (see Deut.
21:18–21). Women are supposed to come to marriage as virgins, and they owe their husbands sexual exclusivity. Laws
against rape and adultery afford women some protection, but
the greater concern of such laws is to protect the father's or
husband's property rights. Men have a virtual monopoly on
the right to divorce, and women normally do not own property. Laws of ritual purity somewhat stigmatize women as
unclean during periods of menstruation and childbirth, yet,
despite these and other official indications of women's second-
class status, many women probably act with considerable
initiative (see, for instance, 2 Kings 4:8–17).

Third, from time to time biblical women step outside
strictly domestic roles and play other roles in Israelite society.
Thus Jezebel and Athaliah rule as strong queens. The wise
woman of Tekoa (2 Samuel 14) persuades King David much as

the prophet Nathan did, and both Deborah and Miriam appear to be prophetesses with political power. It would seem, therefore, that when a woman of powerful personality or charismatic gifts arises, Israelite society allows her to function and enrich the whole community.[3]

Fourth, the Bible occasionally imagines the ideal woman (see, for instance, Proverbs 31), and among her foremost virtues are such domestically desirable traits as being a competent manager. The Song of Songs allows women a frank sensuality, and in the later biblical period, when wisdom becomes a strong interest, the personification of wisdom is feminine (see Proverbs 8 and 9).

Fifth, this feminine dimension to wisdom has a parallel in some of the prophetic language about the collectivity of Israel, leading Frymer-Kensky to speak of "the nonhuman female." In some cases feminized Israel is associated with God as his bride (see, for example, Hosea). The negative aspect of this imagery comes out in passages such as Ezekiel 16, where the infidelities of Israel are expressed as the wanton betrayals of an adulterous wife. Balancing this picture is Lady Wisdom, who is especially pleasing to the Creator God and who wishes to instruct humanity (her children) in the ways of God's teaching. Finally, the overall development of the Bible's sense of God displays a shift from a warrior figure to a nurturing mother whose womb aches with concern for her children (see Isa. 46:3–4 and Jer. 31:20).

Sixth, the New Testament offers evidence that women continue to be subject to patriarchal husbands (see, for instance, 1 Tim. 2:11–12). On the other hand, such influences as Roman law give women new rights in areas like divorce (see Mark 10:2–12). Women are prominent among the disciples of Jesus, and they exercise leadership in the early house churches. Pauline theology (most notably Gal. 3:28) can speak of a radical equality of women with men "in Christ," and the feminine imagery of Revelation suggests that, from early times, the church was considered to be both the bride of Christ and the mother of Christian believers.[4]

Seventh and last, Frymer-Kensky notes that feminist efforts to put aside a patriarchal lens have suggested biblical interpretations according to which women appear less subjugated than traditionally had been thought. Thus Eve is now seen to be quite equal to Adam and capable of initiative or leadership. The female figure in the Song of Songs is another focus of current interest, no doubt because of her equality to the male figure in sensual freedom. Generally speaking, feminist biblical scholarship is interested in trying to reconstruct the likely experience of foremothers, whose contribution to Israel and the church it considers a neglected half of the whole biblical story.

In these seven considerations, we catch at least a glimpse of the main features of women's place in biblical religion. Both the biblical books themselves and the history of their interpretation make woman the lesser sex, but neither the books nor the mainstream of Jewish or Christian theology has foreclosed the possibility that individual women might be holier, wiser, or more instructive than individual men. The radical monotheism of biblical religion, in fact, removes certain stereotypical dangers that afflict nonbiblical religions. For example, whereas the religions of India and China tend to project all of the main disjunctions in human experience and human social roles onto ultimate reality, the bottom line of biblical theology is that God transcends the dualisms of human beings. Of course, biblical theology has to use analogies from human experience and human social organization. Moreover, it tends to picture divinity as male. But the mysteriousness of the biblical God, which Samuel Terrien has captured well in the title of his fine work on biblical theology, *The Elusive Presence*,[5] always puts a firm limit to such depiction. Indeed, the biblical God has such an independence, such a primacy in defining reality and possibility, that on occasion typical thinking falls by the wayside, and a prophet or wisdom writer speaks of God's no more being able to abandon Israel than a nursing mother can abandon her child.

Relatedly, the theology that the Gospels attribute to Jesus so stresses the unconditional quality of God's love that Jesus feels free to deal with women more spontaneously and intimately than the Jewish customs of his time allow.[6] Admittedly, the name that Jesus instinctively uses for God is *Abba,* a diminutive and familiar form of the Aramaic for "father." But we may see in Jesus' whole bearing toward women the assumption that God is their father as much as the father of men. In the Gospel of John such women as the Samaritan whom Jesus meets at the well and Mary Magdalene play the role of apostles, heralding Jesus and the good news to their associates, men as much as women. In the Gospel of Luke Jesus is especially interested in the plight of women and children, because their marginalized status makes them especially dear to God and fit for the graces of the kingdom.

The overall biblical presentation of women is thus rich and capable of development in many different directions. In our reflections on individual biblical passages dealing with women, we shall have full occasion to explore this richness and consider how it may best serve women in the years ahead.

Discussion Questions

1. Sketch the self-consciousness of a woman whose legal status is that of being her husband's property.
2. How has the transcendence of the biblical God limited the patriarchal tendency to depict God as male?
3. Why might it be significant that the Song of Songs makes the woman as freely sensual as the man?

Notes

1. Tikva Frymer-Kensky, "Women," in *Harper's Bible Dictionary,* ed. Paul J. Achtemeier (San Francisco: Harper & Row, 1985), pp. 1138–41 (hereafter cited as *HBD*).

2. See Phyllis Trible, *Texts of Terror* (Philadelphia: Fortress, 1984).

3. See Jo Ann Hackett, "In the Days of Jael: Reclaiming the History of Women in Ancient Israel," in *Immaculate and Powerful,* ed. Clarissa W. Atkinson, Constance H. Buchanan, and Margaret R. Miles (Boston: Beacon, 1985), pp. 15–38.

4. See Elisabeth Schüssler-Fiorenza, *In Memory of Her* (New York: Crossroad, 1983).

5. Samuel Terrien, *The Elusive Presence* (New York: Harper & Row, 1978).

6. See Ben Witherington III, *Women in the Ministry of Jesus* (Cambridge: Cambridge University Press, 1984).

PART 1

Texts from the Hebrew Bible

Introduction to Part 1

Recently I had occasion to reconsider the Hebrew Bible in the context of undergraduate teaching.[1] It was a delightful experience, and I came away with a new appreciation of the humanism and richness of the text. In its three main divisions—Torah, Prophets, Writings—the Hebrew Bible crisscrosses the main provinces of the human heart. Although Sinai and Zion may be the two most important poles, as Jon Levenson recently has argued,[2] a dozen lesser personages than Moses and David cry out for attention. The Bible clearly has come to include whatever the Jewish community considered revelatory. If an incident, a tradition, or a memoir shed light on the nature of the Lord, Israel's God, or on the nature of the Israelite community, it was grist for the canonists' mill. The result is what the anthropologists call "thick" description. Like a painting with layers of color and built-up surfaces, the Hebrew Bible reminds us that communities inevitably add on, correct, reedit, and refocus their understanding of their primordial experiences.

This process apparently went on, first in oral and then in written form, for the better part of two thousand years.[3] If we date Abraham and Sarah to about 1800 B.C.E. and fix the setting of the canon of the Hebrew Bible toward the end of the first century C.E., we find ourselves with that sort of span. To be sure, no one knows what the original form of the traditions about the ancestors was. For some scholars, the historical existence of Abraham or even Moses is quite questionable. What is unquestionable, however, is that first tribes and then a wider people continually thought about themselves and articulated their identity by reference to primary stories about such forebears as Abraham and Sarah, Jacob and Rachel, Moses and Miriam. Eric Voegelin has described the biblical narratives as comprising a "paradigmatic" history.[4] The people who used these master stories were more interested in the

3

patterns they set, the normative configurations they proposed, than in the particulars of the original occurrences. One
need not deny that the biblical writers were rendering the
past as truthfully as they could to insist that they were not
writing what we moderns mean by history. Equally, one can
completely defend their use of myths—stories that slip out of
history and claim archetypal status. Nowadays "myth" is an
honorable category, because literary analysts see that some
kinds of truth can be touched only by stories and symbols that
bypass ordinary, workaday assumptions.

Through its long, fecund incubation, the Hebrew Bible
kept orienting itself by reference to key figures such as Moses
and David and key events such as the giving of the law on
Sinai and the exile to Babylon. The Torah, the first and most
revered portion of the Hebrew Bible, is dominated by Moses.
Because of the influence of Genesis in Western history, we
sometimes forget the primacy of Moses, which is based on a
twofold traditional Jewish assumption. First, Moses traditionally was considered the author of the whole Torah, or
Penteteuch, so that Genesis, as well as Exodus, Leviticus,
Numbers, and Deuteronomy, was thought to have come from
his hand. Second, without depreciating the creation account,
traditional Judaism probably laid more stress on the exodus
from Egypt and the giving of the law on Sinai. These were the
events in which Israel had been created. Certainly Genesis
provided the cosmic background, as well as penetrating insights into human nature and invaluable memories of the
beginnings of the twelve tribes. But most literary analysts of
the Hebrew Bible now think that the Torah became canonical—regulative—for Jewish life only after 300 B.C.E., by
which time the editing of all five books of the Torah was meant
to serve a people struggling to keep alive not so much their
bonds to God the Creator as their covenant with the God of
Moses and David, who they thought had made them unique
among all the peoples of the earth.[5]

The notion of covenant therefore continues to attract much attention from biblical scholars. After showing the precedents for the biblical covenants between the Lord and Israel offered by legal forms of neighboring peoples, such as Hittite suzerainty treaties, scholars note that Israel thought God had claimed her for his own. She was to be his special, unique people, not because of any merits of her own, but because of God's incalculable love. Indeed, as the prophets developed this theme, there was a romantic dimension to the covenant. It was as though God were a handsome he romancing a potentially beautiful but often begrimed she. And this dimension probably was closer to the heart of God's intentions for Israel than the legalistic aspects of the covenant. After all, God did not need a nation of servants to keep his fires fed. He was not like the divinities of the other nations, a force so crude it could be controlled by burnt offerings. Admittedly, Israelite religion sometimes showed signs of that sort of thinking, but its inmost pulse is better rendered by the symbols of romance and marriage.

Prophets such as Isaiah, Jeremiah, Ezekiel, and Hosea make full sense only when one appreciates their struggles to get Israel to appreciate the love that God has lavished upon it. Even the disparate pieces collected in the third section of the Hebrew Bible, the Writings, keep reminding us of this innermost set of covenantal possibilities. Thus many of the Psalms, Ruth, and the Song of Songs speak of love, of fidelity and infidelity. Without the backdrop of covenantal love, even Ecclesiastes and Job lose much of their resonance. Indeed, angular pieces such as Ecclesiastes and Job probably would never have made it into the canon had Israel not been sufficiently confident of its amorous bonds with God to let their challenges to superficial faith be flung down.[6]

At any rate, this is the line of interpretation, the basic assumption, I have found most useful for configuring the Hebrew Bible's texts on women. Unless one allows the Bible its own religious terms, its own convictions about the love God showed Israel in the past and could be begged to show it again, neither the grandeur nor the pathos of biblical women comes clear. On the one hand, they were daughters of the covenant, fully enfranchised members of the people God had espoused; on the other hand, they regularly suffered liabilities, what we might call civil diminishments or incapacities, because of their sex. One must remember that we are speaking of patriarchal times, when women virtually everywhere suffered similarly.[7] Still, it bears reflection that Israel did not think of itself as like the other nations and that therefore all Israelites, daughters as well as sons, had many grounds to respect, love, and even equality. So Jewish feminist theology often finds itself able simply to turn the ideals of its tradition, both biblical and talmudic, against abusive, sexist practices, just as Christian feminist theology often finds itself challenging sexist practices in the church by citing the Pauline assertion in Gal. 3:28 that there should be radical equality.

As the different texts from the Hebrew Bible come before us, we shall have to note the background that scholars tend to assign each and pay attention to its literary genre. Only after having done so can we proceed to work on the text's basic ideas and then assess what they might mean today. What should emerge from our survey of such background, however, is the wonderful diversity of the biblical materials. The Hebrew Bible is certainly a book to confound a simple-minded approach to divine revelation. With wit, argument, memory, appeal to historical precedent, social solidarity, and concern to honor the divine holiness, the Bible plays all the stops on the organ of humanity's interactions with the divine mystery. With appreciation, love, respect, prejudice, abuse, blindness, the Hebrew Bible shows itself a very human work, admirable yet flawed by the finitude and sin our kind show everywhere. So it can be exhilarating as well as depressing to read about biblical women and ponder what their femininity has meant. It can bring us into that best of places—the religious crux where "God" and "human nature" start to become codefining. That place is where religion teachers should keep trying to meet their students.

Discussion Questions

1. How did Israel tend to use its memories of past figures such as the ancestors?
2. What significance did a covenant of love have for biblical women?
3. How do "humanity" and "divinity" both come into focus in the ideal biblical study?

Notes

1. John Carmody, Denise Lardner Carmody, and Robert L. Cohn, *Exploring the Hebrew Bible* (Englewood Cliffs, N.J.: Prentice-Hall, 1988).
2. Jon Levenson, *Sinai and Zion* (Minneapolis: Winston/Seabury, 1985).
3. See Norman K. Gottwald, *The Hebrew Bible: A Socio-Literary Introduction* (Philadelphia: Fortress, 1985).
4. Eric Voegelin, *Order and History*, vol. 1 (Baton Rouge: Louisiana State University Press, 1956).
5. See Brevard S. Childs, *Introduction to the Old Testament as Scripture* (Philadelphia: Fortress, 1979).
6. See Gustavo Gutierrez, *On Job* (Maryknoll, N.Y.: Orbis, 1987).
7. See Gerda Lerner, *The Creation of Patriarchy* (New York: Oxford University Press, 1986).

1

Genesis 2:23–24

Then the man said, "This at last is bone of my bones and flesh of my flesh; she shall be called Woman, because she was taken out of Man." Therefore a man leaves his father and his mother and cleaves to his wife, and they become one flesh.

The scholarly consensus is that this text occurs in a stratum of the J, or Yahwist (J from the German *Jahwist*), tradition. J is the oldest of the traditions woven into Genesis, probably having roots as early as the tenth century B.C.E. It is earthy, shrewd, and the source of some of our most memorable Genesis passages. In contrast to the priestly (P) source that opens Genesis and the Bible, J is less interested in questions of cosmic order and more interested in concrete humanity, with its wonders and scars alike.

Our text occurs in a block of J material extending from 2:4b to 3:24. In terms of the full canonical text, this block, concerned with the creation and disobedience of the first human beings, is in part a reprise of the account of the creation of all the things of heaven and earth (see 1:26–29 for the P account of the rise of human beings) and in part a new venture, a much closer look at the creature of most interest to the Bible. Prior to our verses, the J account has narrated the creation of the earth and the heavens and the formation of the man from dust, into which God breaths the spirit of life. Placed in Eden to keep its gardens, the man is commanded not to eat of the tree of the knowledge of good and evil. At this time he is alone, apparently a solitary male, and the full force of both the Lord's creative force and command rest on him. God then seems to observe the solitary state of this man and to decide it will not do. So, to make him a helper, God fashions beasts and birds of every kind. (In the J account, the man is the first creature; in the P account, human beings come at the end of the creative process.) However, none of these beasts or birds is satisfactory. Apparently, the man needs a different sort of helper.

There follows the well-known story of the formation of a woman from the rib of the man, whom God has put into a deep sleep. When God takes the woman to the awakened man, he utters the words of our text, every indication being that he is delighted, if not indeed awed. The etymology of *woman* clearly derives from *man*, and the story of the rib may be a visual way of putting this derivation. A midrash (Jewish interpretational gloss) on this text offers the opinion that humanity originally was bisexual—an undivided whole.[1] How literally we are to take this opinion is uncertain, but it underscores the mysterious affinity between male and female, which is such as to suggest a common source. The second of our two verses seems in the nature of a homily, a short sermon by way of reaction to the man's exclamation. However, it is a homily with an eye to Israelite custom, as well as the well-nigh universal custom of all peoples: when woman and man marry, they leave (emotionally if not physically) what had previously been their strongest emotional ties: those with their parents. Even when one grants that the extended family structures of the ancient Near East make it possible the author meant to include the new family arrangements set

between the spouses, who become daughter and son to another set of parents, the basic reference to the implications of
heterosexual encounter seems obvious. The two become one
flesh, not just because that is how children get born, not just
because that is what families arrange so that children get born,
but because from the beginning they have been "one flesh" in
the sense of allied, so made physically and emotionally that
"helping" defines their relationship.

This said, we must also underscore the fairly obvious patriarchalism or male supremacism of the text. This stance
seems more unthinking and assumed than deliberately
taught, but it shows quite clearly that the J authors thought of
male humanity as the primary instance and of female humanity as something secondary, if not derivative. (One should not
push images too hard and assume that the woman's coming
from the man's rib means the authors thought in terms of
direct physical derivation.) In contrast, the creation account
in P makes humanity male and female from the outset (1:27).
The idea that women exist to be helpers of men, rather than
independent agents or species of humanity equally entitled to
receive help, buttresses this male-supremacist reading. J
takes us into a patriarchal world in which men place themselves at the center of society (indeed, at the center of creation) and in which women (as well as beasts and birds) exist
for men's support.

Nonetheless, the tone of the man's exclamation softens this
legitimate reading. However much he accepts the notion that
he should have a helper, someone to assuage his lonely estate
as the overlord of God's work, he is delighted beyond the
measure one would expect had he been shown "man's best
friend" or a noble steed. Even were these animals to prove
themselves exceptional helpers, servants willing and able to
labor from dawn to dusk, the man would still be *alone*, the
word that dominates Gen. 2:18, where God is musing about
the situation of his first creature. The helper the man sees

upon awakening from the sleep that allowed the removal of his rib bids fair to dispel his loneliness. Furthermore, we may infer that she seems a work worthy of God, something that can more than redeem the man's loss of part of his bodily substance.

The exclamation thus stresses the unity of the now two examples of humankind. To bone-depth, as something inscribed in the flesh of both, they are together. By cleaving, they make a natural unity, a primordial building block. Indeed, their sexual union will be a reminder of their unified beginnings. Even when the man is made the source of the woman (in an arrogation of birthing symbolism to males that has parallels in other patriarchal societies—woman's primacy in producing new human life is something male-dominated societies everywhere have struggled with), the more important point is the conjunction of their destinies. From the moment the man delights in his womanly helper/companion/ coordinated flesh, their story is bound to unfold as one family tale.

If we now step back to take stock of how this text rings in a feminist age, we realize, perhaps fully for the first time, that the Bible is one of feminists' great problems. For centuries, people have been able to go to this text, usually thinking it virtually God's dictated word (both traditional Jews and traditional Christians tended to think this way), and find an anthropology, an understanding of human nature, that makes masculinity primary and femininity secondary, or ancillary. The tip-off to the patriarchal mentality comes in the biological shift that makes the male the producer of the female. This twist so flies in the face of how every mother's son has come into being that we should hear the alarm bells ringing. Patriarchy felt it had to say that, in the beginning, at the crucial first hour, masculinity begot femininity. After that beginning, the fathers perhaps felt, the helper could take over the ongoing reproduction. The male had given the first initiative, had provided the creative impulse (and had been accorded the first honors), so the patriarchal mythology remained intact.

One notes similar tendencies in such parallel creation accounts as the Japanese. There, in the Shinto chronicles, the male, Izanagi, has to speak first, because that is what is fitting. Because Izanami, the female, breaks this fitting pattern, their first child is defective.[2] On the other hand, in many places the Bible is its own debunker of patriarchalism, including in this text. For it is not the first male who really creates, but only the Lord God. Thus any tendency of patriarchal Israelite mythology to snatch the creative power from females and arrogate it to themselves runs into the textual problem of God's creative primacy. At best the first male was the matter from which God fashioned the first female. A certain male primacy remains, in that the myth first considers humanity to be solitary maleness, but this "advantage" is proven inadequate, unworkable, and so any extended claims to male supremacy easily could be debunked ("When you were on your own, you couldn't hack it"). Throughout, God's judgment and creative power are truly significant, and by the end God has made it clear that authentic humanity is a delightful coordination of male and female.

Insofar as present-day culture allows feminists to start from an assumption that men and women are radically equal in their humanity, it places feminists in a dialectical relationship with the biblical text. We shall see that this is a regular occurrence. Here feminists may judge themselves both debtors to the text for a deep insight into the coordination, the shared origin and fate, of men and women, and people called to accuse the text of patriarchal sexual biases. In other words, feminists may find themselves not only recipients of a valuable heritage but people whom honesty forces to challenge, criticize, and even, at places, reject the biblical text. Such a finding implies the heady wine of critical hermeneutics—theory of interpretation that wants both to listen and to respond. We shall see a good deal more of this need for a critical mind, but here we should mark well the maturity that critical interpretation requires. One cannot do it well as an ideologue, an absolutist. Neither unchallenging fidelity to the letter of the scriptural text nor ungracious refusal to recognize the contributions of biblical faith will do the job. If the text manifestly is inadequate to today's feminists' needs, it remains true that the text has helped millions of men and women, however unknowingly, to cherish one another as flesh of one flesh and bone of one bone.

Discussion Questions

1. What are some of the reasons the authors of Genesis probably placed the first man alone?

2. Can one reduce the relationship of man and woman to a formula of derivation, or is there a mysteriously mutual dependence?

3. How do you judge the balance between the patriarchal tendencies of this text and its egalitarian thrusts?

Notes

1. W. Gunter Plaut, ed., *The Torah: A Modern Commentary* (New York: Union of American Hebrew Congregations, 1981), p. 32.

2. Rysyaku Tsunoda, William Theodore DeBary, and Donald Keene, eds., *Sources of Japanese Tradition*, vol. 1 (New York: Columbia University Press, 1964), pp. 25–26. This story is discussed in Denise Lardner Carmody and John Tully Carmody, *The Story of World Religions* (Mountain View, Calif.: Mayfield, 1988), pp. 441–44.

2

Leviticus 15:19

When a woman has a discharge of blood which is her regular discharge from her body, she shall be in her impurity for seven days, and whoever touches her shall be unclean until the evening.

The great books of Genesis and Exodus do their work through moving narratives. Like grand cinematographers, the authors present epic scenes that move the people through the primeval history, the time of the ancestors, and the dramas of the Exodus and the giving of the law. The main interest is what happens to the people of Israel: where they came from, how they came to reside in the loins of Abraham and Sarah, how they took form as the twelve tribes of Jacob, what God did in freeing them from bondage in Egypt, and how under Moses they gained the covenant that made them distinctive among all the nations of the earth.

Leviticus is different. Most likely fashioned by priestly authors interested in the laws that developed in the wake of the Mosaic covenant, Leviticus assumes the dramatic background and gets down to cases: what does covenantal fidelity mean in the concrete? How ought the covenanted people to comport themselves—eat, drink, sacrifice, and conduct sexual relations? The priestly mind we see in Leviticus shares much with the lawyerly mind of virtually all cultures and eras. Because God was thought to demand behavioral performance and because behavioral performance was something that seemed to admit of regulation, the priests became hell-bent on regulating people's behavior. The reader never knows precisely how successful they were in controlling any given performance. Probably what we see on the books is never a valid indication of what was done in the homes, the places of worship, or the places of business. All the more so is that the case with social groups such as women and children, who had little if any voice in the legislating. But the laws do give us an indication of what one corps of Israel's keepers thought was fitting behavior for a people called to be holy as their God was holy. They do speak to us of Israelite religious ideals and so of how some professionals thought about areas of life that needed special bending to God's reputed will, such as sexuality.

Many scholars think the Book of Leviticus came into anything like its present form only after the disasters of the fall of the Northern Kingdom (Israel) to Assyria in 721 B.C.E. and the fall of the Southern Kingdom (Judah) to Babylon in 586 B.C.E. In a time when foreign disruption of Jewish life threatened to destroy the legal traditions that Jewish religion had developed, priestly lawgivers seem to have redoubled their efforts and narrowed the focus of the covenant so that strict fidelity to the laws it had spawned became the most important, if not the only, way of pleasing God. Indeed, by the end of Leviticus (27:34), all law had come to be represented as the direct commandment of God himself, given for all time on Mount Sinai.[1]

Our text occurs in a section of laws concerned with purity and stretches from 11:1 to 16:34. The bulk of these laws deal with matters of individual purity: what to eat, how to purify the newborn, how to deal with leprosy, and how to offer the sacrifices appropriate in other situations where something untoward or offensive has to be righted. No doubt many of these laws are considerably older than the priestly theology that fits them all into God's address to Moses and the people at Mount Sinai. No doubt many of them originally were not considered such life-or-death matters but rather were a blend of what custom had come to consider prudent and seemly. In Leviticus, however, they seem deadly serious, for in their canonical context they pretend to be part of the constitutional basis of Israelite life: matter given by the divine Lawgiver, who had formed a people he wanted to become holy as he was holy.

Leviticus 15:9 obviously is but a single instance of this legislation and aspect of the Israelite legal mentality, but equally obviously it held great implications, both practical and symbolic, for Israelite women and all who dealt with them. Lest we begin with the wrong perspective, however, it is important to realize that Israelite men labored under analogous purity laws, as we see from the neighboring verses 16–18: "And if a man has an emission of semen, he shall bathe his whole body in water, and be unclean until the evening. And every garment and every skin on which the semen comes shall be washed with water, and be unclean until the evening. If a man lies with a woman and has an emission of semen, both of them shall bathe themselves in water, and be unclean until the evening." It is clear, therefore, that we are dealing with a general mentality regarding bodily fluids, especially those directly related to procreation. Something in the Israelite psyche equated the holiness of God with distance from such bodily fluids. People were "unclean" not in the sense that they had something physically sticky they had to wash away. They were unclean in the sense that they were not fit to come into the presence of the living God, were somehow out of phase with divine holiness. They therefore were to remove themselves from the divine presence (that is, not attend worship services or visit the place—tent or temple—thought to

house the divine presence). As well, they were to avoid physical contact with other Israelites, because a touch could make
those other people unclean.

Women's bodily fluids, however, rendered them more unclean than men's bodily fluids rendered men. This discrep-
ancy was in part due to the difference between the duration of
women's menstrual flow and male seminal emission, but it
seems also to have been a matter of kind. For menstruation
apparently was a major reason women were judged unfit to
become priests and minister in the holy places, and men who
were scheduled to minister in the holy places were forbidden
contact with women, lest they touch a menstruant. Common
sense about the patterns of patriarchal society suggests that
the power vested in the Israelite priesthood was at least as
potent a reason for women's exclusion as their blood, but we
would still be missing something of the ancient Israelite mentality enshrined in this verse if we did not focus directly on the
significance of women's blood.

As a seat of life, blood was in effect tabooed. The blood of
the dead and those slain was polluting, and Israelite dietary
laws sought to remove blood from all meat to be eaten. One
can call the blood of the dead and those slain somewhat
unnatural and sense how a natural aversion to it might have
arisen. One can even sense how this aversion could combine
with a sense of the divine holiness or purity to make blood and
divinity two spheres that people felt ought not to mix. Yet, in
sacrifice the blood of animal victims was given over to the
divinity, so the blood of the animal dead was not a simple case.
Even more puzzling is the case of women, whose natural
biology makes bleeding a regular occurrence. What was the
nature of the uncleanliness associated with such bleeding, and
what did it establish in women's psyches (both those of the
original Israelite women, for whom this legislation was
promulgated, and those of the countless generations of Bible
readers who followed after them)?

We should note, first, that "pollution" may not be the best word to render what the text intends, as "unclean" may not. Certainly both sets of overtones occur, but in many religions the predominant tone is one of moral, if not aesthetic, neutrality. One is talking about a natural force that rightly runs in some channels and causes trouble when it gets out of its bounds and collides with other natural forces. Among American Indians, for example, a major reason for women's seclusion during menstruation was that their life power not run into and so conflict with the killing power of the male warriors. Among ancient Israelites, one can argue that a deep appreciation for the fertility vested in women and expressed in female blood made women beings of special status, beings requiring special treatment.

There remain, however, the negative aspects of seclusion and the many ways that women's bleeding helped a patriarchal society strengthen its impression that women were deviant possessors of human nature. If men were the prime instances of human nature, and men did not bleed every month, it made a certain patriarchal sense to consider women strange, aberrant beings one rightly kept away from the holy business that was most on priestly men's minds. Little of this logic was thought out so clearly, of course, but much of it had powerful effects in the subconscious layers of both the male and the female psyche. For of course women were bound to take in and interiorize the images men were fashioning of them, and even when we give women their due as beings possessed of common sense and a wit ready to debunk those who stereotype them, we have to admit that such an internalization has been extremely influential in almost all cultures, definitely including those with heavy debts to the Bible.

Today, when we tend to think that biology has been accepted and the reforms of biblical religion that have moved in the direction of calling nothing in creation unclean have won the day, Leviticus 15:19 may seem a piece of pure archaism. If we want evidence that should give us pause, however, we need only consider the reluctance with which traditional branches of both Judaism and Christianity (that is Orthodox Judaism and Roman Catholic and Orthodox Christianity) approach the question of women's ordination to the rabbinate or the priesthood. Certainly many negative reasons, historical and theological, are placed on the table, but one wonders whether the deeper reasons, those that operate at the level of basic aversions and inclinations, do not still operate, keeping Leviticus 15:19 quite alive. For such passages of Holy Writ canonized the view that something natural to women, something without which women as we know them on the whole could not be, was especially unsuitable for intimacy with God. Nothing comparable in male human nature brought a similar disabling. The taint of seminal emission could end at sundown. For as long as they bled, women were unclean. Feminists who would revise women's standing regarding religious authority therefore had best take a long look at the symbolic history behind women's separation from the altar. It may well have deeper roots in the psyche than most male authorities hitherto have been able or willing to admit.[2]

Discussion Questions

1. What relation do you see between blood taboos and taboos about death?

2. What does religious "uncleanliness" connote?

3. Why have women been considered unfit for the rabbinate and the priesthood?

Notes

1. See Joshua A. Porter, "Leviticus," in *HBD*, pp. 558–59.

2. On religious purity and impurity, see Mary Douglas, *Purity and Danger: An Analysis of the Concepts of Pollution and Taboo* (London: Routledge & Kegan Paul, 1966), especially chapter 3, "The Abominations of Leviticus." For comparative religious background, see Jean-Paul Roux, "Blood," in *The Encyclopedia of Religion*, vol. 2, ed. Mircea Eliade (New York: Macmillan, 1987), pp. 254–56. Roux generalizes: "The menses are universally considered the worst impurity, due to the involuntary and uncontrollable flowing of blood" (p. 256). On the connections among celibacy, priesthood, and purity, see Edward Schillebeeckx, *Ministry* (New York: Crossroad, 1981). On blood in both biblical and talmudic Judaism, see *Encyclopedia Judaica,* vol. 4 (Jerusalem: Keter, 1972), cols. 1115–16.

3

Deuteronomy 24:1

When a man takes a wife and marries her, if then she finds no favor in his eyes because he has found some indecency in her, and he writes her a bill of divorce and puts it in her hand and sends her out of his house and she departs out of his house, . . .

The Book of Deuteronomy probably took shape in the seventh century B.C.E., was influential in the reforms of King Josiah (after about 621 B.C.E.), and received something like its present shape during or immediately following the Exile (587–539 B.C.E.). Most scholars consider Deuteronomy the beginning of a broad history that continues through the books of Joshua, Judges, Samuel, and Kings. A good conjecture is that, around 400 B.C.E., the present Book of Deuteronomy was separated from this larger ("Deuteronomistic") history and joined to Genesis, Exodus, Leviticus, and Numbers as the fifth volume of what within a century or so was considered the most authoritative traditional teaching: the Torah.[1]

Our text occurs in the midst of various laws attributed to Moses and is included in the lawgiver's address to the people, summarizing the ordinances involved in the covenant made with God in Horeb (the Deuteronomic name for Sinai). The miscellaneous character of these laws may be seen in the fact that prior to these stipulations about divorce comes a regulation about plucking a neighbor's grain, while after them come arrangements for a newly married man to be free of military duty for a year and prohibitions against taking a mill or an upper millstone in pledge for a debt.

The unquoted remainder of our text wanders through further eventualities. What happens if the divorced woman is divorced a second time or if her second husband dies: can she remarry the first husband? The answer is no, because she has been defiled (presumably by the second marriage, although perhaps by the divorce proceedings themselves). My main interest focuses in the first part of the text, where obliquely but clearly we realize that Israelite women could be divorced as their husbands wished—whenever they did not find favor in their husbands' eyes or were discovered to have some "indecency." For the record, we should note that such divorce was one-sided: women did not have a parallel right to rid themselves of husbands who did not find favor or were discovered to have some indecency. We should also note that husbands were obliged to grant wives of whom they wished to rid themselves a bill of divorce so that the wives' new status would be clear (and the wives therefore could marry again).

In its particulars, the full intent of this law seems to be to frustrate the process of women's being pushed out and pulled back by husbands who kept changing their minds. It was considered an abomination for a man to have marital intimacy with a woman, reject her, and then resume such marital intimacy after another man had known her that way. Nonetheless, despite the provisions for clarifying the rejected woman's legal status and controlling the passions of men and women who could not decide whether they wanted to be together or not, the clear implication of the law is that the woman is disposable. Marriage meant no more security than that implied in a husband's favor. If he had a bad day or the wife discovered too late that he was simply immature, she could find herself in deep trouble, half-way out the door.

There is no reason to think that most Israelite men were so changeable or immature, but in fact the structure of biblical society made women captive to men's good sense. No doubt many marriages thrived and much conjugal affection bloomed, but the whole slant of the relationship made women completely vulnerable. Was this simply another half-thought arrangement expressing the biblical patriarchalism, or did biblical men relish the subservience of their women and think it good for women always to be kept on their toes? Who could ever say? In either case, we find another contribution to women's second-class, subjugated status.

For millennia, Jewish women could be divorced as their husbands decided. The law we see here in Deuteronomy no doubt had customary force for hundreds of years before its inclusion in the Torah, and during the postbiblical period it was enshrined in talmudic law, shaping the marital lives of all who lived under halakah (Jewish religious law). The rabbis naturally tried to mitigate the hardships the divorce law could work, doing their best to keep precipitous men from ruining their family lives by fits of bad temper. They also would work on the behalf of women who found themselves in intolerable marital situations, trying to persuade frequently recalcitrant husbands to set the poor woman free. But all of this good work remained peripheral to the basic structure of traditional, orthodox Jewish divorce law. The basic structure was what we see in this single verse: if a woman displeased her husband, she could be summarily dismissed.[2]

We live in a time when many think divorce has become too easy. It is hard for us to appreciate the situation of most women, past and recent, who have lived under patriarchal marital structures much like that of Deuteronomy 24. In traditional Islam and in India and China, for instance, similar patriarchal traditions have held sway, trapping millions of women legally as well as financially and emotionally. Such traditions exert enormous pressure to keep one's mouth shut, develop a pleasing disposition, and prove oneself invaluable by producing the desired number of children and maintaining the desired domicile. The majority of traditional cultures have considered children more the property of the father than the property of the mother, so often children merely tightened the screws. If a woman loved her children, what she might have considered intolerable were she alone became tolerable, since, if she were thrown out of her husband's house, she might lose her children as well. Parallels certainly obtain in our society today, insofar as many abused women do not leave home only because they doubt they could care for their children. But seldom is our domestic law as slanted against women as what we find held true for our biblical predecessors.

If the beauty of the biblical conception of the two-sexed human nature shines in its appreciation of the loving coordination men and women can enjoy, the ugliness of the biblical conception glowers in its unwillingness to grant women any significant independence. And, nowadays, we are bound to wonder whether the Bible's unwillingness to grant women independence does not vitiate most of its beautiful thoughts about them. To be sure, we shall see better texts that represent better intuitions and possibilities. But the general tone of the biblical material is so patriarchal that women just do not emerge as full human beings. They may be as intelligent as men or as brave or as holy or as full of faith, but the biblical legislators simply will not grant them independence like that of men.

The woman we picture being cast out by a husband she failed to please virtually never would have entered on marriage with that man as her own doing. Her parents, primarily her father, would have arranged the marriage, and while, strictly speaking, she could not be forced to marry against her will, in fact her wishes often were not the overriding consideration. The parents were interested in providing for her future and fashioning liaisons with other families. Usually they sought the good of all involved, and often they gained it. But too often a woman found herself living with a stranger she initially did not know how to please and after a while did not care to please. Too often she found herself feeling trapped and panicking as the walls closed in. Neither physical abuse nor neglect nor her husband's infidelity clearly entitled her to a divorce. Regularly she was advised to try harder, to smile and bear it. Too little has changed today. For poor women, especially, things seem much the same. We are not likely to see realized the beautiful potential the Bible finds in marital love until we overcome the Bible's own refusal to grant rights to women equal to men's.

Discussion Questions

1. How hard would it be for a woman not to find favor in her husband's sight or to be found to have some indecency?

2. How significant has been the reservation of divorce rights exclusively to men?

3. What is the relationship between independence and the freedom necessary for profound love?

Notes

1. See Dennis R. Bratcher, "Deuteronomy," in *HBD*, pp. 219–20.

2. On divorce in Judaism, see *Encyclopedia Judaica*, vol. 6 (Jerusalem: Keter, 1972), cols. 122–37.

4

Judges 4:4

Now Deborah, a prophetess, the wife of Lappidoth, was judging Israel at that time.

The Book of Judges contains materials pertaining to the period after the death of Joshua and before the rise of the prophet Samuel. It was a period when various charismatic figures took leadership as circumstances or crises dictated. Early in the monarchical period, after David and Solomon had consolidated rule in the territories of the twelve tribes, these materials were collected and received a first editing. Sometime later, perhaps late in the seventh century B.C.E., they became part of a national history (the Deuteronomistic). After the destruction of Jerusalem in 587 B.C.E., they were re-edited. In the canonical Hebrew Bible, they are part of the second major section, the Prophets. More specifically, Judges is part of the former Prophets—the stories concerning the period before the rise of the great writing prophets (Isaiah, Jeremiah, Ezekiel, and the Twelve), who became known as the Latter Prophets.

Our text occurs in a part of Judges concerned with stories of how God would raise up leaders to liberate the Israelites from foreign oppression. One of the most famous memories was of a victory over the Canaanites led by the prophetess Deborah and the general Barak. Indeed, so important was this story that Judges produces it in two versions, the prose version of chapter 4 and the poetic version of chapter 5. Our verse is the opening of the prose version. After it we learn that Deborah used to sit under a tree, known as the palm of Deborah, and render judgment for people who came to her. In other words, people would ask her to decide disputes, or perhaps to help them choose among different options facing them, and she would oblige. The implication is that she had gifts of discernment—indeed, that she was empowered by God with a spirit of prophecy: the ability to see what was happening, what had to come to pass.

Under the influence of such ability, Deborah summoned the warrior Barak and told him that God was commanding him to lead an army of Israelite tribesmen against the Canaanite enemy. Barak agreed, on condition that Deborah would accompany him to the battle. They went together, and the Lord gave them victory by the stratagem of Jael, wife of Heber, who drove a tent peg through the skull of the Canaanite general Sisera.

The story, both prose and poetic, is rather grisly and depends on ancient biblical notions about warfare. Among these were the notion that God was the first warrior of the people, their champion against (the gods of) their enemies, and that victory came at least as much from divine inspiration as from military preparation and prowess. The story also trades on the presumed weakness of women, finding it remarkable—greatly shaming to the enemy and exalting of the Lord—that victory should have come through Deborah and Jael.

I am more interested in the prophetic status of Deborah than the military background of the story. I take it as significant that Jael would seduce an enemy general and then murder him, but Deborah remains the more intriguing figure. For Deborah was a recognized political leader, while Jael was a woman who in Israelite eyes just acted with great wit and valor in a given crucial instance. Deborah was the one through whom God initiated the war, and initiating the war seems to have been another of her services as a prophetess, a woman chosen by God to communicate the divine will.

The text notes that Deborah was married (an alternate reading of the Hebrew might make her simply a "spirited woman").[1] If so, she probably enjoyed her husband's consent to her working as a judge, most likely because of her manifest gifts. At the least, this account reminds us that the laws constraining biblical women were never the sole determiners of their lives. When they had religious gifts or charismatic powers, women could muster considerable influence. For Deborah, this influence was more official than tended to be the case for later outstanding biblical women. In her time legal duties, military leadership, and prophecy were three recognized foci of religious authority. The story implies that she shared in all three forms of authority, in that she decided disputes, called the people to war, and was regarded as an oracle of the divine will. No matter how patriarchal the culture of her time, it could not deny the Lord's use of her. When God chose, patriarchalism had to give way.

We see, then, a conflict at the heart of the biblical notion of authority. On the one hand, the laws and established structures of Israelite life claimed to have come from God and to enjoy divine sanction. Indeed, the effort to consolidate most if not all laws and established structures in terms of the Mosaic legislation was precisely an effort to sink them into the bedrock of the divine will. On the other hand, various prophets or charismatics also claimed authority from God, and the people tended to give them a hearing. The God of Israel was not distant or abstract. To the popular mind, divinity meant power, illumination, a force near and able to effect desirable change. And this God had shown himself no respecter of human judgments. Just as he had led the Hebrews out of

Egypt, in a victory that must have astonished Pharaoh, so he could choose the most unlikely heroes, even women, to save his people in new situations. At such times, the patriarchal structures had to give way. Something closer to the raw divine power was in play: God's direct choice of a leader to inspire.

The history of biblical religion shows us many inspired women, both before the close of the biblical canon and afterward. Esther is like Deborah and Jael in freeing her people from bondage. The Virgin Mary is filled with a Holy Spirit bent on freeing all people from the bondage of sin. Most of the female saints are also charismatic personalities—people who exert their influence through spiritual force rather than organizational office. Being prophetic, we might say, is natural to female sanctity. Although patriarchal males overall have turned their backs on women's leadership gifts, God has refused to make do with only a half a compliment of servants. Whenever God wished, history has seen prophetic females raise up their voices to warn their times of God's will.

Certainly I follow most feminists in thinking that sexual equality means equal access to institutional office and power and that we will have no fully healthy religion as long as women's gifts do not have the potential to weigh as heavily as men's. But until that parousiac day, we do well to appreciate the prophetic, charismatic mode in which many women make their contributions. Nowadays, for example, we see feminism generally allied with the forces that oppose nuclear proliferation and environmental degradation. And even though women are prominent on both sides of the struggles over abortion and the right to life, usually their conflicts boil down to a different ranking of two rights or goals that both sides consider desirable: women's freedom to control their reproductive faculties and preservation of the unborn. What all feminists assume and insist upon is women's full capacity for inspiration—becoming empowered by their own wisdom and God's light to discern the path to justice and peace.

In that context, Deborah is encouraging and instructive. Though she may have first been seen as a helper to a man, and though menstruation made her unclean, and though she could, if married, have been divorced when she lost her husband's favor, none of these or her other liabilities unfitted her for the most important human task, that of being filled by God's Spirit and so commissioned to lead God's people. Deborah teaches us that this calling has always been the most important human task, the most useful human gift: mediating divine light, life, and love. Like the hundreds of charismatic women nurtured by the left wing of the Protestant Reformation, she reminds us that God finds female nature no great liability. God's Spirit breathes where it will. Forebears such as Deborah are solid warrant for our believing today that God's Spirit is as likely to be moving in female hearts and minds as it is in males.[2]

Discussion Questions

1. Does serving well as a judge involve stereotypically feminine gifts?

2. How does Jael break stereotypes of both femininity and biblical morality?

3. Does prophecy involve a sexual component?

Notes

1. See J. Cheryl Exum, "Deborah," in *HBD*, p. 214.

2. On the experience of the Holy Spirit, see Yves Congar, *I Believe in the Holy Spirit*, vol. 1 (New York: Seabury, 1983).

5

Ruth 1:16–17

But Ruth said, "Entreat me not to leave you or to return from following you; for where you go I will go, and where you lodge I will lodge; your people shall be my people, and your God my God; where you die I will die, and there will I be buried. May the LORD *do so to me and more also if even death parts me from you."*

The Book of Ruth is a short story mainly concerned to supply a link in the narrative of the lineage of King David. It probably is quite old, dating between the tenth and eighth centuries, and perhaps it was connected with such ancestral stories as the cycle about Joseph.[1] The story shows how the fidelity of Ruth and Naomi gains them not only security but a place in God's plan, for Ruth becomes the great-grandmother of King David.

Prior to our text, a grim stage has been set. During the time of the judges famine lay hard on the land. A native of Judah named Elimelech went abroad to Moab to try to improve his luck. But he died young, leaving his widow, Naomi, with two sons. The sons took Moabite wives, Ruth and Orpah, but the sons also died. So the three women found themselves alone, without the men they needed to be secure in a patriarchal society. Naomi gave her daughters-in-law leave to return to their native Moabite houses and seek new marriages. She herself planned to return to Judah. Both daughters-in-law initially promised to go with Naomi, but she remonstrated with them to be sensible. Orpah kissed her and left, weeping for Naomi's grief. Ruth clung to Naomi, uttering the words of our text.

At first glance the words seem simply a moving expression of daughterly devotion, and in fact they represent the first good news Naomi has heard in a long time. On further examination, as we shall see, they reveal greater theological depth. For the moment, however, we need to sketch the completion of the story. Naomi and Ruth do return to Bethlehem in Judah. There Ruth gains the favor of Boaz, a kinsman of Naomi, and eventually marries him. This relationship gives both Naomi and Ruth security, and when Naomi holds in her arms the fruit of Ruth's union with Boaz, her kinswomen gather round to praise God for having so dramatically reversed Naomi's fortunes: "Blessed be the LORD, who has not left you this day without next of kin; and may his name be renowned in Israel!" (Ruth 4:14).

Our verses, containing Ruth's profession of fidelity to Naomi, often are cited in expositions of the remarkable friendship that develops between the two women.[2] And, indeed, after these verses, when Naomi accepts Ruth's dedication, the two women share not only home but fate, working together to seize the opportunity offered by the appearance of Boaz and together maneuvering through several difficulties until they see the child who so clearly signifies their success. But the pledge itself is religiously remarkable, because in it Ruth completely throws in her lot with Naomi's faith. A Moabite, Ruth presumably had her own gods and religious ways. She would not have been obliged to drop them because of marriage to Naomi's son, let alone after his death. So her dedication to Naomi is extremely radical: thenceforth, they will share one fate, will commit themselves to the same ultimate mystery. Naomi's people with be Ruth's people. Naomi's God will be Ruth's God. If they are to live, it will be together. If they are to die, it will be to lie in the same grave. To Jews reading of their pact, one of the main marvels would have been the love and wisdom of this pagan Moabite. By the grace of God, she had chosen to join the chosen people. Indeed, she had joined at ebb tide, when fortunes were darkest. What an example she gave of daughterly devotion and religious discernment! How fitting it was that God should have honored her by making her an ancestor of his great favorite, King David!

Beneath the sometimes merely fashionable talk about women's bonding and friendship, feminists now grope after models of women's religious bonding, of their friendship in God. Such searches could do much worse than to concentrate on Ruth and Naomi. The women join forces, weeping and rejoicing as one. The older accepts the younger and offers suitable guidance. The younger reveres the older and provides the energy and fertility they need. Significantly, they forge their bond in great freedom. Naomi does not want Ruth clinging to her out of either a false sense of duty or an inability to go her own way. Indeed, like a guru testing a prospective disciple to make sure the disciple is serious about wanting to venture upon the way, Naomi orders Ruth off. But Ruth will not be deterred, as the genuine disciple will not be deterred. Ruth has seen something in Naomi, has felt something from Naomi's God, that has shone with the luster of pearl. She knows this something—love, faith—is well worth struggling for. She is confident it will outweigh the misfortune and uncertainty that prosecuting it may entail.[3]

The short story turns out well, of course, and at the happy ending we are allowed to think that God has rewarded the women's mutual fidelity. But long before the fruition of their hopes in the child who becomes the grandfather of King

David, the women have started to enjoy success in their venture. By bonding together, weeping and laughing together, they immediately begin to cut their fears down to size. By trekking back to Bethlehem side by side, they greatly diminish the hardships of the journey. Simply by being together, by opening their hearts in mutual love, they have gained a pearl of great price. The happy aftermath is but a fitting setting from which their love can the better shine.

Causes can bring people together. Working for admirable ends does tend to help people clarify their like-mindedness, does put them in a light that makes them especially attractive. To be serious, such work has to want genuine success and not be simply playacting. Like Naomi and Ruth, friends who are also collaborators need to be handling matters of moment, work and decisions that make a difference. Only when they feel they are entering a relationship that is significant both in time and in meaning do their innermost hopes and needs become manifest. But it also seems true that friendship to the degree suggested by Ruth and Naomi requires a religious agreement. Without a union of mind and heart about ultimate matters, a common surrender to divine mystery, two potential friends are unlikely to sound the depths of their possibilities.

If this observation about friendship is accurate, the controversies between religious and irreligious feminists only gain in pathos. No doubt we shall never completely remove them, especially when they occur over such volatile matters as abortion policies. But I hope we can make progress in minimizing them and seeing the losses they cause and the opportunities they foreclose. If nonreligious feminists sometimes have the gifts of passion for political, here-and-now aspects of justice, religious feminists sometimes have the gifts of longer perspective and greater sensitivity to questions about the beginning and beyond—not just of temporary movements but of human existence itself.[4] When one or the other is enjoying an irenic day, this contrast would seem matter for fruitful exchange and mutual supplement. One sister so clearly has her feet on the ground that she forces, ideally gently, the other to remember how much God cares for social justice, how primary are the rights of the poor. The other sister so clearly has been called to wisdom, contemplation of the nonpragmatic questions whose neglect leaves us in a bog of nondirection, that, if she can make herself heard, if others will lend her an ear, their activist struggles to make a better world can start to flow into the general process of redemption. Such a sister helped by such a sister is like a strong city, a completed circle. In their mutual give and take, both/and gradually replaces either/or, to the better health of all.

Naomi and Ruth probably were not identical in their needs and talents. They too probably had different gifts to offer, different gaps to fill. But contemplating their success, their ability to let love take first place and differences come second, could serve feminists of all persuasions a valuable lesson. The crux of the friendship of Naomi and Ruth was their mutual regard and shared fate. Each agreed that the other was precious. Both agreed to stick together, come what might. And so we celebrate them as heroines of both faith and feminine friendship. Like all gracious heroines, they bow to our applause, but I also hear them saying, "Go thou and do likewise."

Discussion Questions

1. Does Naomi's being in dire straits make her more or less open to friendship?
2. Why did Ruth so completely throw her lot in with Naomi?
3. What does the story imply about God's uses of human love?

Notes

1. See Edward F. Campbell and Peter J. Ackroyd, "Ruth," in *HBD*, p. 886.

2. See Phyllis Trible, *God and the Rhetoric of Sexuality* (Philadelphia: Fortress, 1978), pp. 166–99; Susan Niditch, "Legends of Wise Heroes and Heroines," in *The Hebrew Bible and Its Modern Interpreters*, ed. Douglas A. Knight and Gene M. Tucker (Philadelphia: Fortress, 1985), pp. 451–55.

3. See the brilliant commentary by Cynthia Ozick, "Ruth," in David Rosenberg, ed., *Congregation: Contemporary Writers Read the Jewish Bible* (New York: Harcourt Brace Jovanovich, 1987), pp. 361-382.

4. See Eric Voegelin, *Order and History*, vol. 5 (Baton Rouge: Louisiana State University Press, 1987).

6

1 Samuel 1:15

But Hannah answered, "No, my lord, I am a woman sorely troubled; I have drunk neither wine nor strong drink, but I have been pouring out my soul before the Lord.*"*

The books of Samuel form an important block in the Deuteronomistic history. Their special concern is the rise of the monarchy with Saul and David. While materials such as those of our text may represent memoirs from the eleventh century B.C.E., the editing of the books of Samuel probably took place during the Exile (sixth century B.C.E.). As their name suggests, these books take shape by reference to the prophet Samuel, the last of the judges before Israel decided to have a king like the other nations. Samuel stayed famous in Israelite memory as both the prophet who anointed Saul king and the representative of an older, perhaps better premonarchical order. Like Deborah, Samuel represented charismatic authority—direct inspiration by God. With the monarchy, Israel risked trying to institutionalize God's leadership. From the outset of these books, therefore, the authors or editors are at pains to show the favor God had placed on Samuel.[1]

The context of our verses is that Hannah, the destined

mother of Samuel, has been sorely tried by barrenness. The single most important achievement of any biblical woman was to produce children, especially males. We saw signs of this evaluation in the story of Ruth: the fruit of Ruth's union with Boaz was both the sign and the substance of God's favor. As happens to many biblical women, Hannah's barrenness wins her the derision of her cowife, here named Peninnah. Her husband, Elkanah, favors Hannah, yet he is so impressed by fruitfulness that he seems bound to praise Peninnah and frequently to hurt Hannah's feelings. So Hannah is driven back on her deepest resources. Expressing her bitterness to God, she vows that, if God grants her a son, she will dedicate the child to God's service. Our text occurs after the priest Eli has observed Hannah pouring out her heart to God. Because she was moving her lips but making her prayer silently in her heart, Eli thought she was drunk. Hannah hastens to assure him that what he beholds is not a drunken woman but one sorely troubled. She has lost herself in prayer, because of her great need.

The Lord does answer Hannah's request and blesses her with a son. The priest Eli gives her the assurance her prayer would be heard, and she departs in peace, as though conception had already occurred. When it comes to dedicating the newborn child to God, Hannah cries out the song that Luke uses as the basis of Mary's Magnificat: "My heart exults in the LORD; my strength is exalted in the LORD. My mouth derides my enemies, because I rejoice in thy salvation. There is none holy like the LORD, there is none besides thee; there is no rock like our God" (1 Sam. 2:1–2). The rest of the song continues in the same spirit, blessing God, who favors the poor, the weak, and the righteous but overturns the wicked, the proud, and those who trust in their riches or fertility.

Two aspects of Hannah's story clamor for comment: first, her heartfelt prayer; second, the reversal of human judgments she finds typical of God. Both suggest women's stake in liberation theology.

Hannah's prayer goes right to God, pouring out her grief, even her bile. She does not think of prayer as a tidy exchange or a proper little colloquy between herself, a genteel lady, and God, a Victorian parson. Her prayer is herself. If she aches, she cries out painful words. If she is angry, her emotions boil over. For, her God is her life, her vitality. Otherwise, what use has he, what significance? Biblical prayer regularly has an urgency, a high quotient of emotion, that separates it from our present-day approaches to God. Abraham haggles with God over Sodom (Genesis 18). Deborah sings of bloody victory much like a banshee (Judges 5). Neither is concerned with propriety. Both give God what they are at the time of their outcry.

Hannah gives God her need and dereliction. She is at the end of her rope and has nowhere else to go. The fact that later, in the happy aftermath, she also goes to God, this time to praise, shows that her God is not merely a plugger of gaps, a last resort never visited until crisis hour. But she does not blush to beg God for help. If asked how she could humiliate herself to carry on like a drunken woman, she would have been amazed: where else ought a person in extremis to go? How else ought a sufferer to demand God's attention? Compared with her need for a child, Hannah's dignity or need for reserve were as nothing. The implication might well be that, because she held nothing back and took down all shields, God could help her easily.

The second aspect of Hannah's story, her association of God with a justice quite different from that of the world's high and mighty, of course fits in with her hopes. Insofar as she considers herself poor and needy, she longs for God to be a foe of her oppressors, a fighter for people like herself who suffer unjustly. Her instinct, sharpened by suffering, is that, if God merely rubber-stamps the status quo, God has little to offer the majority of people. Virtually everywhere, the many have been at the bottom of the social pyramid, and the few wealthy have been at the top. What sort of God would be interested only in the few? What sort of holiness would give its backing to the powerful and wealthy, who so often have gotten their gains by ill means? A God worthy of Israel's traditions, Hannah is sure, inclines to the side of the poor. As in the Exodus, when God sided with the Hebrew slaves against the mighty Pharaoh, God wants to right the injustices that mottle most social life, to heal the cancers responsible for so much pain.

Liberation theology, both that coming from Latin America and that from other sources, takes texts such as the song of Hannah and the Magnificat of Mary as strong warrants for its convictions. When the Latin American Catholic bishops came to speak of a preferential option for the poor, they felt themselves authorized by such texts. The beatitudes Jesus uttered in the Sermon on the Mount go in the same direction. The suffering servant of Isaiah and Jesus himself on the cross are in the nature of confirmatory seals. When God enters into history, taking up a position of solidarity with humankind, divinity, above all, makes itself compassionate and becomes our fellow sufferer. The liberation of the poor, the ignorant, and the sick is at the heart of the divine work. Redemption, salvation, and liberation are but different names for the same divine intention. At the synagogue in Nazareth, at the outset of his ministry, Jesus put it in words Hannah would have loved to hear: "The Spirit of the Lord is upon me, because he has anointed me to preach good news to the poor. He has sent me to proclaim release to the captives and recovering of sight to the blind, to set at liberty those who are oppressed, to proclaim the acceptable year of the Lord" (Luke 4:18–19).

As liberation theology develops its initially somewhat limited focus, so that spirituality becomes the regular complement of political analysis and action, the prayer of Hannah and those like her should receive as much attention as their hopes for God's reversal of society's historic injustices.[2] The poor whom liberation theology finds to be the apple of God's eye are not limited to either those who pray or women, but it makes sense to consider prayerful women their fine exemplars. For who are a majority of the poor, if not women and children? And who are the majority of those in the church pews, telling their beads or murmuring over their Bibles, if not women? The women at the cross of Christ, like the women who gather in the plazas of Latin American cities to protest the disappearance of those the dictatorships consider threats, sum up in their substance humanity's proper stance before suffering and evil. On the one hand, they are racked by pain, scored to the bone by concern for their children and other loved ones. On the other hand, they are implacable, resolved never to say to Caesar the yes they owe only to God.[3] Hannah initially was concerned mainly about her own misfortunes. When the priest Eli came upon her, she was close to neurosis from self-concern. By the time of her canticle of praise to the God who gives salvation, her horizon had expanded. She had learned that her sufferings were far from unusual, that God's care had to be spread far and wide.

The most mature religious feminists mirror this pattern of development. As they work and pray, they find their personal pains and their own hopes for liberation echoed from a thousand other witnessing posts. So their feminism, their championing of women's full humanity, helps them sense that people of color and people on the margins of society for whatever reason represent claims upon God similar to their own. Everywhere, a good God interested in fertility ought to be overturning unjust structures, fulfilling the life-or-death needs of the many. Hannah's prayer therefore might be a model for religious feminists: "O LORD of hosts, if thou wilt indeed look on the affliction of thy maidservant, and remember me, and not forget thy maidservant . . ." (1 Sam. 1:11).

Discussion Questions

1. Why was Hannah so distressed by her barrenness?
2. In what sense was Hannah's prayer emotionally honest?
3. What are women's special needs for liberation?

Notes

1. See P. Kyle McCarter, Jr., "Samuel, the First and Second Books of," in *HBD,* pp. 902–4.

2. See Gustavo Gutierrez, *We Drink from Our Own Wells* (Maryknoll, N.Y.: Orbis, 1984); Rosemary Haughton, *The Passionate God* (New York: Paulist, 1981); Sebastian Moore, *Let This Mind Be in You* (Minneapolis: Winston/Seabury, 1985).

3. See Robert McAfee Brown, *Saying Yes and Saying No* (Philadelphia: Westminster, 1986).

7

2 Samuel 14:13–14

And the woman said, "Why then have you planned such a thing against the people of God? For in giving this decision the king convicts himself, inasmuch as the king does not bring his banished one home again. We must all die, we are like water spilt on the ground, which cannot be gathered up again; but God will not take away the life of him who devises means not to keep his banished one an outcast."

The two books of Samuel form a single literary unit. Among the major subdivisions are the story of Samuel, part of which we considered when contemplating Hannah; the story of the election and rejection of Saul; and the story of David, including both his rise from simple shepherd to king and his reign. Second Samuel 9–20 is a high point in biblical literature, probing the psychology of David and creating perhaps the most memorable Old Testament personality. Our text occurs after the famous incident of David and Bathsheba. Also preceding our text is the rape of Tamar, daughter of David, by her half brother Amnon. To avenge Tamar, Absalom, David's favorite son, has Amnon murdered, after which he flees the king's court. So 2 Kings has shown David to be deeply flawed: an adulterer, a murderer (of Bathsheba's husband, Uriah), and a father who alienates his son (Absalom) because he takes no swift action to punish his daughter's rapist.[1]

Joab, David's right-hand man, perceives that the king would like to be reconciled with Absalom but does not know how to accomplish this. So Joab gets a woman renowned for her wisdom to approach the king with a petition. Her story is that one of her two sons has killed the other and that she is being pressured to surrender the killer for vengeance. For her to comply would leave her doubly bereft, so she asks the king to intercede to stop the next bloodshed. King David agrees. Our verses express the shift by which the woman applies David's judgment to his own conflict with Absalom. Just as the prophet Nathan had gotten David to see the evil of slaying Uriah by telling David the parable of the little ewe lamb (2 Samuel 12), so the wise woman presses him to see that vengeance against Absalom is as unacceptable as forcing a mother who has lost one son to lose a second.

We may note, first, that the woman accuses David of having planned "such a thing" (the death of the best heir to the throne) "against the people of God." Several implications bristle in these phrases. "Such a thing" is to be more interested in punishment, the letter of the law, than in mercy and good sense. It is to continue old ways of blood feud, a life for a life, that ill fit the existence created by the covenants (Mosaic and Davidic alike). "The people of God" deserve better, should do better. God has not treated them according to strict laws of justice and vengeance. If God had, who could have survived? Instead, the watchword of the biblical God is his steadfast, merciful love (*ḥesed*). Can the king not see that this dispensation of grace applies as much to his own flesh and blood as it does to the son in a story of a strange woman who comes pleading?

One can almost see the woman raising a frail fist to threaten the king out of his obtuseness. Joab may have gotten her to play this role of provocateuse, but she has made it her own. Her verdict on the king—that, in his decision for her, he convicts himself—rings with authority. The wisdom attributed to her has produced a doughty self-confidence: she is sure of the role she is playing and can enact it with conviction.

I am also taken with the woman's poetic, if dour, turn of phrase: "We must all die, we are like water spilt on the ground." Human mortality had made a deep impression on her (perhaps she is aged). In its light, time seems too short and life too precious to waste on vengeance. The fragility of life should indeed guard us against sentimentality. No doubt the woman had seen enough in her years to keep the pursuit of any criminal, even the king's son, in perspective. But she is still convinced that God wants life rather than vengeance, that God is eager to reward those who act mercifully and preserve life, because that is God's own way. These convictions enable the woman not only to play her part well but to dot the i's and cross the t's so that the king cannot miss her meaning.

The episode of "the wise woman of Tekoa," as she is known, is sufficiently convoluted to admit of several interpretations, but for our purposes those I have sketched will do. For the woman has accepted the role of being a champion of mercy, a debunker of the harshness that treats life cheaply and is willing to toss it away to satisfy hurt feelings. In fact, the woman easily becomes an everywoman, a common citizen, who has become disenchanted with the once great king and judges his weakness—his lack of resoluteness—the cause of the country's imbroglio. But one cannot separate the king's weakness from his history with Bathsheba. Had he not been in the wrong regarding her (she became his queen and the mother of Solomon), he would have had the moral stature to rebuke Amnon and so perhaps head off the rupture with Absalom (there were other factors, so the rupture may have been inevitable). Had he not been flawed in his dealings with women generally, going back to Michal, the daughter of Saul

(2 Samuel 6), he might have treated Tamar much better. As it was, Tamar seems barely to have existed for him. The rape she suffered upset David, irritated him, but he felt little outrage. So the woman of Tekoa may suddenly have found herself fed up with the king, despite all his status, and emboldened to give him a piece of her mind, as though he were a foolish son of her own.

Women have inherited such a courageous, debunking, and accusing role as one of their socially sanctioned possibilities. Dorothy Dinnerstein has dealt with this role, tying it to her generally pessimistic view of the "sexual malaise" that has warped most of the interactions between men and women.[2] Although in most cultures women have been kept from making history, men have often sought women's approval and tolerated women's scorn. In part both sexes have simply been prolonging the role mothers play in small boys' games of war and destruction. In part women have been forging a way of keeping their sanity: though I cannot change this deadly, wasteful way men have constructed war and law, I can at least mock it and preserve my soul.

Still, male-dominated history has brought women large measures of grief. All of the children mangled by guns and swords had been carried by women. Most of the tears shed at premature funerals have rolled down women's cheeks. The woman of Tekoa gains much of her plausibility from this historic pattern. Like many other influential women, she plays the petitioner's game, sticks to the rules of the marginal, but internalizes none of it. With little to lose and full awareness that it is bad form in most societies for powerful men not to seem gracious toward women, such women have spoken freely. Now and then, a man like David, who is still open to God's voice in his conscience, makes their risks worthwhile.

David hears the woman of Tekoa, as he had heard the prophet Nathan. He remains the man who can be struck to the heart with repentance. That does little for Tamar, but it does profit Absalom. The woman's intercession has gained Absalom a reprieve, which unfortunately he does not use wisely. Nonetheless, it is instructive for us to ponder what intercessions like that of the woman of Tekoa have accomplished throughout the ages. Again and again, they have been a way for antagonists to put aside ego, drop their demand for bloodlust, and be reconciled. Mothers mediating between fathers and sons, sisters mediating between brothers, teachers and nurses smoothing rough interactions—all have helped keep the world from becoming totally a war zone. To be sure, sometimes women have been bitter and unforgiving. Sometimes they have refused reconciliation and kept old wounds fresh, as though they loved the taste of hatred. But on the whole, women's instinct has been to resew connections, redo at least the surface amenities so that life can proceed without violence and unpleasantness. I think that such work has made many women unsung peacemakers, children of God.

Discussion Questions

1. The king was God's anointed authority. Where did the wise woman of Tekoa get the courage to approach and accuse him?
2. Why have women so often debunked male competitiveness and violence?
3. How central is reconciliation to the will of the biblical God?

Notes

1. See Phyllis Trible, *Texts of Terror* (Philadelphia: Fortress, 1984).
2. Dorothy Dinnerstein, *The Mermaid and the Minotaur* (New York: Harper & Row, 1976). Also instructive on this theme is Robert Coles and Jane Hallowell Coles, *Women of Crisis*, 2 vols. (New York: Delta/Seymour Lawrence, 1978, 1981).

8

1 Kings 19:1–2

Ahab told Jezebel all that Elijah had done, and how he had slain all the prophets with the sword. Then Jezebel sent a messenger to Elijah, saying, "So may the gods do to me, and more also, if I do not make your life as the life of one of them by this time tomorrow."

After David and Solomon, the kingship went to pieces. The northern and southern portions of the land became two realms, and the regular refrain of the biblical chronicler is that both the kings and the people did what was evil in the sight of the Lord. Above all, they withdrew their loyalty from the one God of the covenant and ceased to practice the social justice dictated by the covenant law. The Deuteronomistic theology sees such evil as the reason for the misfortunes that plagued the land. Eventually, both the North and the South fell to foreign aggressors, in what much biblical theology regards as punishment for their sins.

The spokesmen for God who denounced such sins were the prophets. The most famous of the early, nonwriting prophets was Elijah, who worked in the first half of the ninth century B.C.E. At this time the unjust king Ahab was being maneuvered by the even more wicked queen Jezebel. Jezebel was a

49

foreigner, a Phoenician princess much committed to the gods—baals—of her native land. The contest between the God of the Mosaic covenant and the baals became deadly serious, as we see in our verses. Elijah has bested the prophets of Baal (the summary of the foreign deities) and so infuriated Jezebel. She promises not to rest until Elijah's blood runs, and to the biblical author's mind her hatred for the Lord whom Elijah serves makes her name a synonym for wickedness. At the least, then, she is a good antidote to any temptation to think biblical women all sweetness and light.

Jezebel finally came to a bad end, her flesh eaten by dogs (2 Kings 9). In the sight of the biblical authors, her death was simple justice, as it was simple justice for priests of the false foreign gods to be slain. How much in these stories is genuine history and how much parable is hard to say. Jezebel died, though, as she had lived, a robust hater, and the biblical authors especially stigmatized her because she was a foreigner and a woman. Under both headings, they saw her a seducer. By the time the Deuteronomistic history entered the biblical canon, Israel was trying to reconstitute its national life after return from exile. Foreign elements seemed to threaten its historic relationship with God, so the reformers Ezra and Nehemiah proscribed marriage with foreigners. Jezebel, like the foreign wives of Solomon, made useful propaganda. Representing femininity turning all its wiles against God and luring Ahab (her obvious inferior in intelligence and will) to his doom, *Jezebel* encapsulated in one word the worst scenario the reformers could envision. Thus, she greatly helped their cause.

These are rather obvious dynamics in the Jezebel stories. More subtle are the plays on fertility religion and the insinuations that femininity is opposed to the true God. The baals of Israel's neighbors were functional deities, much concerned in the popular mind with keeping the natural world running. Storm and rain, sun and warmth, expressed their powers. If one wished fertility, prosperity, good dealings with nature, one would cultivate the baals. Canaanite and Phoenician religion therefore represented a stage of human consciousness at which nature and divinity were still compactly joined. Most people could not conceive of power and vitality apart from nature's cycles.

In contrast, the God of the Mosaic covenant was so authoritative that nature could not capture him. From the account of creation in Genesis to the strange naming of God in Exodus 3 (where Moses learns only that God is as God will be experienced to be by sharing time with him), the Lord whom Israel was to worship transcended natural forces. The experience of the exodus from Egypt should have taught the Israelites once and for all that their God was unique, but each generation seemed on the verge of sliding back into the easier, more spontaneous association of divinity with nature. The horror the prophets saw in this view was the loss of a God who could save human beings from nature's caprices. If divinity were nothing more than the amoral ambiguity of natural processes, human beings were at the mercy of irrationality. But if the Exodus was the tip-off to God's nature, divinity was a liberating love, a steadfast care.

Bonded to such a divinity in trust, the prophets considered Israel the beneficiary of a gracious covenant. An Ahab threatened to pollute the covenant by his religious dullness and injustice. A Jezebel was worse, for she threatened the entire meaning of Israelite history. If her policies held sway and were not fought tooth and nail, the Exodus and the true God might vanish from popular consciousness. Prophets such as Elijah called on God to prevent this catastrophe. We may wish they had not been involved in such a crude conflation of faith and bloodshed, but we have to see that, in their eyes, idolatry was an effort, however unknowing, to slay both the Israelite people and their God.

The connections many cultures have made between women

and nature play into the biblical animus against Jezebel.[1] These connections usually rest on the perception that women have a biological clock fixed to the cycles of the moon and that women usually resist harsh dichotomies between matter and spirit. Such periodicity and holism appear more "natural" than the abstraction and dichotomizing to which men in many societies have been prone, and insofar as those societies have been patriarchal, men have made themselves the keepers of higher culture (which preeminently has been religious law and cult). Women in turn have been associated with nature and lower culture, if not carnality.

These associations work in the symbol that Jezebel became. Seductress of Ahab, defender of fertility religion, hater of the prophets (who represented higher Israelite culture), she offered patriarchal biblical religion a handsome target. Perhaps she was indeed the hater of God the books of Kings portray, the epitome of injustice and slaughter. But her female sexuality lent this recipe spice, even venom. Misogyny, rooted in the primordial otherness of female sexuality, kept dancing at the edge of the authors' consciousness, tempting them to blame this *woman* for the wickedness of the realm. Jezebel the person may well have merited the obloquy the text gives her. Whether Jezebel the woman has deserved the place accorded her in the history of symbols is another matter.

The prophet Elijah is a winning character, above all when we meet him just after our verses, at the mouth of the cave to which he has fled from Jezebel. There he encounters a God who seems to tailor divinity to the prophet's harried spirit. Elijah's God is not in the wind, the earthquake, or the fire (as the Mosaic God had been). Elijah's God comes after all this stormy display, speaking in a still small voice. Jezebel has been seeking the prophet's life. God gives him back his life, his vital spirit, by leading him into a silence more significant than all the noise and violence. The cave perhaps symbolizes depths of existence Ahab and Jezebel, the baals and other natural forces, cannot sound. The main danger in this reading comes when we make such a spiritual capacity something Elijah the male has and Jezebel the female could not have. Fortunately, the Bible itself, as well as common observation, avoids such an inference. Indeed, as we shall see, the Bible, if anything, risks stereotyping divine wisdom, the play of God's Spirit, as feminine.

Thus, we leave Jezebel, thinking she can provoke quite complicated thoughts about the nature of the biblical God and the feminine symbols of evil. Insofar as nature, beguilement, and religious hatred present themselves in feminine garb, Jezebel is a dangerous sister. Beyond the deserts of her deeds, she can swell to archetypal proportions. And then, like Eve, she can cast a shadow on all powerful women, who tend to be punished more than their plain sins deserve. As Eve became a more negative symbol than Adam, so Jezebel became a more negative symbol than Ahab. Each may in fact have been the stronger literary figure, but neither proves that female nature begets more religious problems than male nature does.

Discussion Questions

1. What was the main conflict between Jezebel and Elijah?
2. Has the image of Jezebel outrun what the biblical texts justify?
3. Are women more "natural" than men and so a source of special difficulty to biblical religion?

Note

1. See Sherry B. Ortner, "Is Female to Male As Nature Is to Culture?" in *Woman, Culture, and Society,* ed. Michelle Z. Rosaldo and Louise Lamphere (Stanford, Calif.: Stanford University Press, 1974), pp. 67–87; Carol P. MacCormack, "Biological Events and

Cultural Control," *Signs*, Vol. 3, No. 1 (Autumn 1977), pp. 93–100; Rita M. Gross, "Menstruation and Childbirth as Ritual and Religious Experience among Native Australians," in *Unspoken Worlds*, ed. Nancy A. Falk and Rita M. Gross (San Francisco: Harper & Row, 1980), pp. 277–92.

9

Esther 4:15–16

Then Esther told them to reply to Mordecai, "Go,
gather all the Jews to be found in Susa, and hold a fast
on my behalf, and neither eat nor drink for three days,
night or day. I and my maids will also fast as you do.
Then I will go to the king, though it is against the law;
and if I perish, I perish."

The Book of Esther probably derives from the fourth century B.C.E., when the Jews were living under Persian rule. It
has long functioned as part of the feast of Purim, which
celebrates the deliverance of Jews of the eastern Diaspora
from persecution. While legendary, Esther functions on the
model of Deborah, Jael, and other biblical heroines, risking
much to save her people.

The story concerns the fate of Jews living under the Persian
Ahasuerus. Esther, a beautiful Jewish maiden, has become
one of the king's queens. The wicked Haman, a leading Persian official, plots to destroy the Jews. Esther's guardian,
Mordecai, opposes Haman and pressures Esther to use her
influence with the king on her people's behalf. Our text gives
Esther's decision. Although no one is to enter the king's
presence unbidden, under penalty of death, Esther will take

the risk. The king welcomes her handsomely, and she is able not only to save her people (and Mordecai, who is under sentence of death) but also to destroy Haman. Known in Hebrew as Hadassah, Esther became the heroine of Purim, celebrated each year for her bravery and beauty.

Our text has some interesting features that perhaps go below the legendary strata to whatever was the historical core of the Book of Esther. First, there is the allusion to fasting. The point clearly is preparation for something serious, dangerous, and needing God's special help. Mordecai previously had been going about in sackcloth and ashes, bewailing the promised destruction of the Jews. Esther's action is less grandiose but similarly dramatic. To convince Mordecai, the other Jews, her maids, herself, and God of the seriousness of the situation and her proposed course of action, she calls for a general fast. In their bodies, all involved are to realize the peril and so wholeheartedly petition God's help.

Second, Esther decides to go to the king, using her status as a favorite queen in the royal harem. Nowhere does the text moralize about this situation. It is taken as a fact of life in imperial Persia, something Jews had to handle as best they could. Like it or not, Esther's beauty had won her the king's attention. Mordecai's appeal to her to use this fact had been twofold. She owed it to her people to do what she could on their behalf, and she deluded herself if she thought her queenly status would save her when the persecution against the Jews broke out. She was in a position to help, which perhaps was providential—the reason God had given her beauty and eased her way into the king's favor.

Third, Esther accepts Mordecai's arguments and squares her shoulders to the task. Certainly she was used to following Mordecai's behests, for he was her guardian. But now she has come of age, and no one can tell her how best to handle the king. For that she has to rely on her own instinct. Something must have told her there was a chance he would be glad to see her and so waive the rule against unbidden approaches. In the midst of what on the whole is a sexist story, Esther takes an independent stand. (Esther gets the chance to become a queen because Vashti, the former queen, is removed for diso-bedience—she refused to come when summoned by the king. This refusal was bad enough in itself, but the court's greater worry was that it would set a precedent and women throughout the realm would start disobeying their husbands.) She will use her brains and beauty both; she will take her life in her hands; but Mordecai and the other Jews had best realize the high stakes in the game she will be playing. By ordering them to fast, Esther makes the scene thoroughly her own.

This story is one of several in the Bible that underscore the theme of divine providence. Esther's final words rely on di-vine providence: if she is to perish, so be it. Joseph in Egypt displays a similar theme: God drew good out of the wicked-ness of the brothers who had abandoned him to death. But Esther confronts her possible death more directly than Joseph did. She finds that, whether she lives or dies, she belongs to her Lord. This attitude perhaps frees her to be especially effective in her interview with the king.

Anyone interested in feminist spirituality has to be on the alert for decisions, techniques, even moods that conduce to inner freedom and so outer effectiveness. Much of the key to deepened "spirituality" lies in our sense that, if we pay atten-tion to experience, both our own and what others report, and discipline ourselves to follow what past experience seems to dictate, we get better at our job of loving God and loving other people. When we become serious about the spiritual life, we quickly realize that, while God alone gives the grace that produces success, we ourselves have an important say. Yet, much of our say boils down to predisposing ourselves to receive God's grace—to recognize it, respond to it, second it. Increasingly, I suspect that God's grace trades in the coin of freedom. The more we can drop our compulsions and fears, the better able we become to feel God's love and extend it to others. In this connection, false worries, foolish regrets, and useless defeatism seem the paramount enemies. Esther found a way to banish them. Her way invites further reflection.

If we perish, we perish—that is Esther's stark philosophy. Face the worst case, confront the fullest debacle, and half the problem will be solved. What if we fail or even die? We certainly have failed before, and if our project is significant, surely it is worth the risk of failing again. Death is nothing to risk casually, but on the other hand, death is the one surety in every life, bound to come sooner or later. So if the cause is important enough, risking death makes great sense. The mothers who confront the Latin American butchers must think this way. That must be how one thinks when working with an underground—a network dedicated to resisting Nazi, Soviet, or other brutalities. In our own land, it must be how one thinks when nuclear arms or racial prejudice stands revealed as naked evil. If one perishes in opposing them, so be it. Not to oppose them would be to lose one's soul, a far worse kind of death.

I favor neither easy talk about risking life nor hyperbole about the ruthlessness of the unjust powers of one's society. In times of relative peace, in societies of relative decency and justice, easy talk and hyperbole disserve good causes. Even in deadly serious matters, such as the conflict over abortion policy, they obstruct progress and risk obscenity. All the more are they out of place in discussions of women's ordination, lesbian rights, or sexist prejudice in the marketplace. All of these matters indeed reveal deep injustices, ugly sins, outright evil. But God has tolerated a world, decided to share a world, rampant with what ought not to be. And God's comportment, according to Jesus and the other biblical exemplars, shies away from easy talk and false drama. God's grace, making the exemplars free, tends toward humility and matter-of-factness; it says, "Here's what has to be done; let's do it."

If we perish in certain spiritual or political ventures, so be it. If we do not venture, we shall perish by default. Not to choose is to choose. Not to go forward, not to keep struggling, is to go backward and defect from God. At the base of a straightforward, somewhat minimalist spirit, the divine inspiration shows in a widening freedom. Then what the authorities say (the church leaders, the talky pundits) works less restriction. Even what the sisters say and the ideological voices of the self tend to fade. The silence of God is more persuasive. The freedom to love and do what one wills is more significant. Certainly one must stand up and be counted, but it matters less who does the counting or how many points the self-appointed umpires award. If we are able to plant and water while leaving the increase to God, we can share Esther's realism. What will be after we have done our best will be. Which of us can add an inch to our stature or direct the wind where to blow? Not even Solomon in all his glory looked as good as a lazy lily. Activists may see only business in Esther. A wiser reading comes away with more nuance: she left the deepest part of her business in the hands of her God. I think Esther would have liked the advice of Teresa of Avila, another no-nonsense woman: Let nothing disturb you.

Discussion Questions

1. Do fasting, sackcloth, and ashes have any relevance today?
2. Is it ironic that a harem queen should have become the Jews' deliverer?
3. Is "If I perish, I perish" the same as "Let nothing disturb you"?

10

Jeremiah 31:20

Is Ephraim my dear son? my darling child? For the more I speak of him, the more do I remember him. Therefore, my womb trembles for him; I will truly show motherly-compassion upon him. Oracle of Yahweh.[1]

Jeremiah is a good representative of the Latter Prophets. He worked in the seventh and sixth centuries B.C.E., witnessing the fall of Judah to Babylon. Few prophets have spoken more eloquently about the burdens of being God's mouthpiece, and few have been more poetic. The present book shows signs of considerable reworking and editing. On the basis of what probably were oracles of Jeremiah himself, disciples of both Jeremiah and Deuteronomistic theology refashioned what became a Jeremiahan collection. The first twenty-four chapters feature visions, prophecies of judgment, and laments—most of them suiting a time when defeat and punishment by Babylon were becoming ever more likely. Chapters 25–45 contain more personal materials that seem to reflect the prophet's own religious experience. In their midst occur oracles of restoration and comfort such as our text. These passages make most sense as efforts to console those exiled to Babylon and depressed by captivity. How much they have been influenced by the freedom from captivity offered by the Persians in 538 is unclear, but they make the overall theology of Jeremiah a sophisticated blend of warning and encouragement.

The warning is the easier to understand, since it was a stock theme of both prophetic faith and Deuteronomistic theology: sin will win you stern punishment. The encouragement moves in the deeper waters of grace: Israel must remember that God has always loved it for his own inscrutable reasons, and these reasons have not vanished simply because Babylon has crushed it.

Our text is an outstanding example of the prophetic insight into God's unmerited love. Many metaphors described the relationship between God and Israel, covenant and marriage among the most influential. A third metaphor was that of parenthood. Israel was the child of God. In our text this metaphor of parenthood takes a distinctly maternal cast. As Phyllis Trible, whose translation I have used because it brings out the precisely feminine imagery much better than the Revised Standard Version, explains:

> Yahweh speaks here of the divine inner-parts trembling for Ephraim the child. In some other passages, the word *inner parts* parallels *womb* (Gen. 25:23; Ps. 71:6; Isa. 49:1; cf. Ruth 1:11). Hence, the first colon of this concluding line can be appropriately read "therefore, my womb trembles for him." Support for this translation comes in the second colon, where the root *rḥm* appears in two verbal forms. Thus an exclusively female image extends its meaning to a divine mode of being: "I will truly show motherly compassion upon him," says Yahweh. Furthermore, these two verb forms parallel the verb forms of the preceding line. Together they emphasize the tender memory and the earnest love of Yahweh: "I do remember him lovingly" (v. 20b); "I will truly show motherly-compassion upon him" (v. 20c). In summary, strophe four is the voice of Yahweh the mother. Parallels between Rachel and Yahweh

occur in each of its three sections. . . . Yet there is a difference. The human mother refuses consolation; the divine mother changes grief into consolation. As a result, the poem has moved from the desolate lamentation of Rachel to the redemptive compassion of God. Female imagery surrounds Ephraim; words of a mother embrace her son.[2]

The result of this imagery is that God becomes a leading biblical woman. Certainly a few texts do not change the predominantly patriarchal cast of biblical theology. Male imagery continues to prevail. But the prophetic theology, seeking the best security human experience allows one to imagine in God, breaks the stranglehold of male imagery and shows us several new implications of the divine love.

First, the divine love is tender and nonjudgmental. Whatever harshness may have been appropriate when Israel was cavorting about, puffed up in its pride and heedless of God's demands for exclusive worship, has softened. Looking on the battered Israel, God sees a child wounded and fearing it has been abandoned. Like a mother moved to the deepest part of her being, pained to the womb where the child was formed, God feels compassionate love. Isaiah had said God could no more abandon Israel than a nursing mother could abandon her child (49:15). Jeremiah feels the same. Israel had been to God like a child conceived in her womb, carried many months, brought forth in anguish, and nourished at the breast. What mother could look on one she had so brought into being and not be pierced by its sufferings? When they sought desperately to relieve the agonies of the Exile, the greatest prophets felt their spirits move to this logic of maternal love. God had expended too much on Israel's behalf, had given too much of the divine substance, for Exile to be the last word. The pains Israel was suffering had to resound in the divine center like the birth pangs of yore and so set up sympathetic vibrations.

The second implication of this theology, more apparent to later readers than to the prophets themselves, was God's transcendence of all metaphor and imagery. No single set of symbols could ever capture the divine essence. To get the best picture of God they could, theologians would have to employ the richest possible range of human experience. Obviously, therefore, they would have to employ the experience of the feminine side of the race. This included women's experience of romantic and maternal love, but also men's experience of being moved to tenderness and compassion. By implication, it carried the warning that each sex was as human as the other and that full humanity, let alone full symbolism of divinity, had to provide for the full range of experience, emotion, and insight labeled feminine.

In tracing out such implications, we have wandered into the fertile field of theological creativity; namely, the question of where we get our senses of God.[3] Aware of how influential popular theology is when it comes to people's self-images, feminists have long fought the patriarchal tendency to cast God as a supermale. Looking at history, they have concluded that, if God is male, the male tends to be god. Men have indeed held the majority of power, even in situations when the Great Goddess was the major deity or females were nearly as prominent in the pantheon as males. But the most oppressive cultural situations for religious women have been those in which both divinity and the social order have been patriarchal.

When we take Jeremiah and Isaiah as warrants for developing a theological femininity, we begin to consolidate both sets of implications. We get images and conceptions of God more amenable to women's experience and feminists' conviction that full human health demands the acceptance of a human reality that is two-sexed right down to its foundations.[4] And we get freedom from the tyrannies of sexuality, patriarchal or feminist, which come from forgetting the divine transcendence of our limitations as women and men. God has modes of loving that even the fullest appropriation of human experience cannot fathom (perhaps cannot even imagine). For instance, God has to be loving through the flux of the tides and the shifting of the tectonic plates. Insofar as we have not appreciated this natural, impersonal aspect of divinity, we have not developed the theology of nature and ecological sensitivity we need.

More politically, the difference between even our best symbolism for God and the divine love ought to buttress Paul's ringing conviction in Galatians 5:1: "For freedom Christ has set us free." Because the male is not God and the female is not God, males and females alike ought to be able to represent God, serve God, and lead God's people. Equally far from God and equally potent sources for intuitions of the divine love, both women and men ought to be accounted credible witnesses, intrinsic authorities, by the simple evangelical test: by their fruits you will know them. The tender love Jeremiah intuited came to focus in the lovely figure of a divine mother moved to her womb. When this intuition has received its due, been accounted as important as the figures of the divine king and husband, we will have a considerably better theology of redemption than we have had in the past. As well, Christians may have a much richer trinitarian theology. The prophet has opened the door. Feminist theologians would be wise to start entering in.

Discussion Questions

1. What was the connection between the Exile and Jeremiah's imagery of the divine womb?
2. Would anything substantial change if Jeremiah's God were mothering a girl child?
3. Why do many women find a feminine God a great benefit?

Notes

1. This translation comes from Phyllis Trible, *God and the Rhetoric of Sexuality* (Philadelphia: Fortress, 1978), p. 45.

2. Ibid.

3. See John Bowker, *The Sense of God* (Oxford: Clarendon Press, 1973).

4. See Rosemary Radford Ruether, *Sexism and God-Talk* (Boston: Beacon, 1983).

11

Proverbs 9:1–2

Wisdom has built her house, she has set up her seven pillars. She has slaughtered her beasts, she has mixed her wine, she has also set her table.

Among the books of the Writings, which constitutes the third portion of the Hebrew Bible, Proverbs, Job, and Ecclesiastes usually are considered "wisdom literature." About this literature Roland E. Murphy recently has written: "The origins of Israelite wisdom are presumed to lie in the insights, oral and written, of the family and clan and also of the wise men who could have provided training for courtiers in Jerusalem. The existence of some kind of 'school' may be inferred from similar institutions in Mesopotamia and Egypt. Wisdom, in fact, is an international possession, cultivated throughout the ancient Near East."[1]

Among the traits that Israelite wisdom literature regularly displays are little reference to the covenants, a focus on the lessons of experience, concern about retribution (punishing the evil and rewarding the good), and the use of brief, pithy sayings. Proverbs differs from Job and Ecclesiastes in being more optimistic that the evil will be punished and the good rewarded.[2]

Although Solomon became the archetypal wise man and so traditionally was considered the author of Proverbs, most scholars take the present work as a set of collections of prudential sayings, some of them attributed to otherwise unknown sages such as Agur and Lemuel of Massa (see 30:1 and 31:1). This summary collection probably dates from the postexilic period, perhaps late in the sixth century B.C.E., but undoubtedly individual sayings are much older, some probably stemming from monarchical circles in the tenth century B.C.E. Many of the proverbs have the overtones of instruction for youths. Our text occurs near the end of the first collection in Proverbs (chapters 1–9), which is mainly poems about wisdom.[3]

Several of the poems personify wisdom, and regularly the persona is feminine. The gender is clear in our text and in such others as 7:4 ("Say to wisdom, 'You are my sister'"). It is implicit in another famous text about wisdom, where she is the firstborn of God's creation: "The LORD created me at the beginning of his work, the first of his acts of old. Ages ago I was set up, at the first, before the beginning of the earth. When there were no depths I was brought forth. . . . and I was daily his delight, rejoicing before him always, rejoicing in his inhabited world and delighting in the sons of men" (8:22–24, 30–31). Biblical thought sometimes portrays a divine aspect in this way, here wanting to distinguish between God and the wisdom by which creation occurred but not knowing how to distinguish without dividing them. So here the figure is of a delightful playmate, a goodness of mind that gave the divinity much pleasure. The New Testament writers had such a conception of wisdom in mind when they thought about the Logos, the reason of God become manifest in Jesus the Christ. As the power and wisdom of God, Jesus somewhat fit the feminine persona of the wisdom of Proverbs.

In our text wisdom is more domestic, a sort of holy hausfrau. She has built her house, whose seven pillars give it a palatial look. She has prepared food and drink for a banquet. In most of the wisdom literature, wisdom is a prudential matter: knowing how to live well. Most likely the subtlety and grace of such prudence contribute to its having (in many cultures) a feminine persona. Here the biblical writers drive the point home by presenting wisdom as a gracious and generous hostess. She knows how to run a household and manage a fine party. More significantly, she provides people lovely housing and attractive nourishment.

These latter qualities I find worth meditating upon. A mainly intellectual wisdom might well be concerned with the order of the universe, the objective "way things are." Then, those possessed of such wisdom are able to live realistically. Here wisdom is more visceral, somatic, gustatory. I am reminded of the wordplay in Latin: *sapientia* (wisdom) is cognate to *sapor* (taste). In other words, wisdom is something savory. A person is to taste the goodness of the Lord. Knowing God's love ought to bring one delight. Meditating on the law of the Lord day and night ought to bring one deep fulfillment—the sort of contentment that comes after an excellent meal. The very first psalm in the Psalter speaks in this vein. Many scholars put it in the genre of wisdom psalm, and interpreters interested in the canonical structure of the Psalter point out that it orients the whole collection of psalms toward a worship that would be wise.[4]

Many women spend significant portions of their lives focused on care and feeding. As mothers, they nurse children and prepare the family meals. As nurses, they supervise the rehabilitation and nourishment of the sick. As teachers, they feed young minds. No wonder psychologists of female moral development such as Carol Gilligan find that girls place considerably more importance on care and relationship than boys do.[5] Women's spirituality is wise to take such psychological findings to heart in refashioning the traditions spawned by the Bible so that they better serve women's typical patterns of growth.[6] Without tying women's wisdom to running house-holds, feminist theologians might well muse about the spiritual nourishment women provide and need.

To find satisfaction in God, one needs much more than information, more even than solid intellectual formation. Important as these are, they merely serve what is the heart of the religious matter: loving communion with God. Whether through contemplative prayer or a service that builds up the community, especially by helping the poor and the suffering, the saints commune with God. For them love palpably is the pearl of great price, and they make little distinction between love of God and love of neighbor.

The two loves illumine one another. We learn about the deepest possibilities in human love by taking to heart the love of God manifest in Jesus, the saints, and our own best experiences. By risking human love, we learn how God might feel about us and be serving our good.[7] And all such love, of God or of fellow human beings, is holistic: a matter of the whole mind, heart, soul, and strength. All is subject to the vicissitudes experienced by the lovers in the Song of Songs. It has periods of delight and complete satisfaction. It has periods of loss, feeling bereft, thinking the lover has departed forever. Under such motifs, however, runs a less dramatic but ultimately more significant theme of nourishment. The love of both prayer and service of one's brothers and sisters feeds the soul. It keeps one going, for better or worse, for richer or poorer, in sickness and health. As the Song of Songs realizes toward the end, love is even our antidote to death: "Set me as a seal upon your heart, as a seal upon your arm; for love is strong as death, jealousy is cruel as the grave. Its flashes are flashes of fire, a most vehement flame. Many waters cannot quench love, neither can floods drown it. If a man offered for love all the wealth of his house, it would be utterly scorned" (8:6–7).[8]

In our text, a womanly wisdom offers in love all the wealth

of her house. She wants to feed the hungry, to educate the "simple," who have no notion what the love of God, and so human prosperity, requires. Her delight is with the children of women who take the divine word to heart and find nourishment, who drink at the fountains of tradition and slake their souls' thirst. Such children grow strong and healthy. They can withstand the assaults of the fools who say in their hearts there is no God. They can distinguish between solid food and that which has been adulterated. In a dozen housewifely images, new masters of the spiritual life might show wisdom, God's Holy Spirit, busy about women's work. Although we take it for granted, such work is the most basic service human beings render one another: birth, feeding, clothing, health care, emotional support. God's wisdom above all shows in such service. The knowledge we should most associate with theology, divine science, is what one has to know to nourish life. Laying her table, getting ready to feed her guests, welcoming them to the house of God, Lady Wisdom offers feminist spirituality a solid touchstone: Whatever provides nourishment and makes people at home in God's house befits and bespeaks God's delightful playmate.

Discussion Questions

1. Why is biblical wisdom more practical than speculative?
2. What are the main sources of religious nourishment?
3. How useful for feminist spirituality are symbols of nourishment and caring?

Notes

1. Roland E. Murphy, "Wisdom," in *HBD*, p. 1135.
2. Ibid.

3. See Roland E. Murphy, "Proverbs," in *HBD*, pp. 831–32.

4. Brevard S. Childs, *Introduction to the Old Testament as Scripture* (Philadelphia: Fortress, 1979), p. 513.

5. Carol Gilligan, *In a Different Voice* (Cambridge, Mass.: Harvard University Press, 1982).

6. See Joann Wolski Conn, ed., *Women's Spirituality* (New York: Paulist, 1986).

7. See Sebastian Moore, *Let This Mind Be in You* (Minneapolis: Winston/Seabury, 1985).

8. See Samuel Terrien, *Till the Heart Sings* (Philadelphia: Fortress, 1985), pp. 29–49.

12

Proverbs 31:10

*A good wife who can find? She is far more precious
than jewels.*

At the end of Proverbs we find another poetic section, this
time in praise of the ideal wife. It has become the staple
encomium to the Jewish woman, telling us much about the
Bible's view of marriage. Our text is the opening anthem.
Following it come such wifely attributes as winning her husband's trust, bringing him gain, working diligently at crafts
such as spinning, obtaining good food, supervising the maids,
buying and planting fields, working late into the night, caring
for the poor and needy, providing her household warm
clothing, dressing herself well, enabling her husband to sit
among the important men of the land, selling productive
goods to merchants, bearing herself with strength, dignity,
and confidence, speaking wisely and kindly, and being
blessed by her children and husband. The finale of this extended, poetic burst of praise is worth quoting: "And he [her
husband] praises her: 'Many women have done excellently,
but you surpass them all.' Charm is deceitful, and beauty is
vain, but a woman who fears the LORD is to be praised. Give
her of the fruit of her hands, and let her works praise her in
the gates" (31:28–31).

Today this text is bound to make feminists feel ambivalent. On the one hand, there is a recognition of all the competence and hard work that domestic management can entail. This ideal wife is busy, efficient, and productive. She probably would be a demon of energy, and the implication is that she cares for her family's every need. As well, she is wise, kindly, concerned for the poor, and beloved by her husband and children. To efficient management she adds qualities of mind and heart. This record is no mean accomplishment, and such a woman undoubtedly would be strong and self-confident.

On the other hand, much of her status seems auxiliary. The text implies that her diligence supports her husband's more public affairs, her care enables her children to live well, perhaps even to be spoiled. This wife is not property, but she is a good investment. With her as a helpmate, a husband will get a good return. The last lines of the text also are jarring. Why need charm be deceitful? Does a good wife have to be a plain-Jane? Why does the author insinuate a fear of beauty? Can we not praise beauty as a gift of God and so love it that it has little temptation to be vain? It is fine to praise the fear of the Lord. Any creature of wit bows down before the awesome divine mystery, the daunting divine holiness. But surely fear of the Lord is only the beginning of wisdom. Surely as wisdom matures it comes to appreciate the gratuitous love that makes God put aside lordship and deal with us as a mother struck to the core, as a lover desiring our beauty.

In a single text, then, we find the ambiguity of the heritage bequeathed women by the Hebrew Bible. Even at its moments of high praise, the Bible reflects a man's world. From the Eve created as the helpmate of Adam to the good wife who eases the life of her senatorial husband, woman is the second sex. This patriarchal view is simply not acceptable. If the Bible cannot sponsor a radical sexual equality that wipes out "first" and "second," it fails to provide what both women and men require today. Today both sexes require help in fashioning a discipleship of equals. Under God, women and men need to grow in partnership, friendship, mutual help, and warm love. The love the senatorial husband might feel for the industrious wife of course could be genuine and warm. In private life they might play and commiserate as equals. But the structures of marital and social life in their time shunt them away from such equality. So do the religious structures of most societies, including our own.

Unless it became possible for women to be the senators, known at the gates and sitting among the elders of the land, the society of the ideal wife's time would not measure up to the full potential of the covenant. That is a lofty ideal, of course, but what lesser goal or attainment is worthy of the covenanting God? Similarly, until the Judaism and Christianity of our latter days become assemblies where men and women are full equals, they will continue to fail the covenants. Why should rabbis or priests be only men? Why should women be most of the auxiliaries, the beloved helpers? Nothing essential to being a good rabbi or priest is sex-specific. Nothing essential to being a good auxiliary is sex-specific. Industry and wisdom know no sexual boundaries. Neither does serving as one of the elders, the political leaders, of one's land or religious community. It is time we trashed all the phony rationales that keep women from doing and being whatever they want as freely as men can. We must honestly admit that they are really rationalizations. People of religious wisdom know that the authority worth cheering is intrinsic: shown by intelligence and goodness. People who insist on extrinsic criteria for religious authority, who do not admit the primacy of the Holy Spirit, show themselves to know little about the spiritual life. One may sympathize with their deficiencies, as one would with a person crippled in other ways, but one cannot take them fully seriously or not lament their accession to leadership roles.

From a feminist perspective on wisdom, it is hard not to

become depressed by the mediocrity, the religious obtuseness, of most religious leadership. Letting Jewish, Protestant, and Orthodox feminists speak about their own traditions, I shall limit myself to Roman Catholic religious leaders. A few distinguish themselves for their intelligence and depth. The American bishops as a whole deserve applause for their pastoral letters on peacemaking in a nuclear age and on the American economy. They may also deserve applause for standing up to Rome concerning both rights of conscience in general and rights of bishops in particular. But even when one has tried to second every good initiative and appreciate every real difficulty, the formal, hierarchical leadership is disappointing. Compared with what a cadre of wise women might accomplish, or even with what a cadre of wise men might accomplish in an atmosphere of freedom, the bishops fly the colors of mediocrity. Few if any are evil or malicious men. Too many are dullards—D students, party hacks, people promoted because they will not question the party line or rock the boat. My church is not a place where excellence is rewarded. It rules out women and married men for leadership roles, sinfully diminishing its talent pool. The wonder is that it functions at all. There must be a Holy Spirit.

But why should the people of God have to tolerate dullards and mediocrities? Why should the freedom for which Christ has set us free mean less than maintaining the party line? Such an inversion is perverse. Such quenching of the Spirit makes one think the Spirit has never been known. I realize that the history of the church proves enthusiasm, charismatic movements, lay leadership, and the like have had their problems. I have no illusions that, if my church said "Fiat lux" and opened orders to women and married men, it would inaugurate the Parousia. But I have run out of excuses for the arrogance and obtuseness I see crippling diocese after diocese. I have few tears left for so culpably stupid a leadership. Again and again, it fixates on sex and ignores life. Time after time, it seizes up with fear—or is it cowardice? Does it not know that God is running the world and that Christians are definitely in the minority? Does it not see that honesty and love, the only quintessentials, breathe where the Spirit wills? And how long will it be before servanthood becomes more than a tired if not hypocritical slogan, something to be acted out on Holy Thursday and ignored or not understood the rest of the year? These are not matters of recondite theology, of esoteric political shrewdness. These are the ABC's, the things that leap off the gospel pages.

So give us fewer paeans to good wives, fewer dutiful acknowledgments of women's important and special gifts, fewer tortured defenses of policies simply wrong and dumb. In their place, just a little courage, a little imagination, a little wit, and a little resolute honesty would be like fresh air from on high. Indeed, charm can be deceitful and beauty vain, but both also can be gifts of God. Bishops can be wise and self-spending, but bishops also can be pains in the soul. Let us start judging and promoting all of the people of God, men and women alike, only by their fruits. I believe Jesus thought that this test was fundamental.

Discussion Questions

1. Why was the ideal biblical wife so industrious?
2. How should one regard charm and beauty?
3. Why are so many religious authorities mediocrities?

PART 2

Texts from
the New Testament

Introduction to Part 2

The New Testament presupposes the Old Testament. Virtually everywhere the Law, the Prophets, and the Writings form the backdrop. What we have seen about biblical women from the Hebrew Bible therefore should serve us in good stead.

The books of the New Testament all stem from a period of about fifty years—roughly 50 to 100 C.E. The earliest New Testament writings come from the apostle Paul, but certainly memories of Jesus and collections of his sayings that have found their way into the Gospels antedate what we find in the first Pauline writings. The literary priority of Paul should be a salutary reminder that the churches that produced the Gospels already were living an intense life pivoted on the risen Christ. The historical priority of the Jesus who did mighty deeds of healing, preached poetic and biting messages about the Reign of God, died on the cross, and was raised by the Father should be a salutary reminder that Jesus of Nazareth was the inspiration and the final explanation of every New Testament page. We cannot know this historical Jesus except through the impression he made on those who wrote the Gospels. We cannot know the risen Christ of the early churches' experience except through the impression he made on Paul and the other New Testament writers. And all of our knowledge, of course, is colored by our own time and religious experience. Still, just as the stories of the Old Testament prove wonderfully diverse and challenging, so do the stories of the New Testament. New Testament woman is as intriguing a figure as Old Testament woman.

The two women are sisters through their common faith in the God of the covenant. Both Jewish and Christian women are daughters of this covenant, children of grace. If they differ about the significance of Jesus—whether he was or was not the Messiah—they can agree about the God whom Jesus called Father. Everything come down from this God, this Father of Lights, is gracious. In all places and at all times, the most relevant question to ask is how God is showing the divine love. Believing in this love, recalling such paradigms as the Exodus and the Resurrection, women of biblical faith have ample reason for thinking themselves blessed. Compared to the gifts of the covenants, what they have to suffer from human folly is secondary, often almost inconsequential.

The New Testament is also indebted to Hellenistic culture, as were such portions of the Old Testament as the wisdom literature. The Pauline and Johannine writings, especially, are concerned with displaying Christ as the power and wisdom of God. As well, the New Testament is concerned with social structures drawn from Hellenistic culture. Jewish cultural patterns certainly have left their mark, but so have the patterns of the Gentiles (especially the Greeks and Romans) contemporary with the New Testament writers.

Concerning women, Tikva Frymer-Kensky notes a shift during the New Testament period.

> While there are indications that patriarchal rules were continued among Christians (e.g., I Tim. 2:11–12; but cf. Eph. 5:22–24, where submission of wives is under the rubric that all are to be subject to one another in Christ, v. 21, including husbands, v. 25, who are to imitate Christ's self-sacrificing love toward their wives), there are also indications that the role of women was influenced by the non-Jewish environment of early Christianity.[1]

Specifically, some texts assume women to have had the right to initiate divorce, and several mention women as prominent church leaders.[2]

Nonetheless, the various "house codes" we find in the New Testament reflect the Hellenistic subordination of women to men. It is assumed that men are the heads of the households and that women owe men obedience. Thus such materials as the Pauline and Pastoral Epistles, which often are dealing with Gentile churches in a Gentile environment, show patriarchal structures parallel to those of the Gospels, where the prevailing cultural influence was Jewish. From both fonts of cultural influence, women got the message that they were the second sex.

The center of the New Testament, as I have implied, is Jesus himself. Although he began as the proclaimer (of the Reign of God), after his death he became the one proclaimed: the heart of the gospel. Thus Paul preached Christ crucified, while Mark, Matthew, Luke, and John wrote various prologues to the passion story. Each of these authors was a Christologist, an interpreter of the significance of Jesus of Nazareth. From a combination of common memories and traditions peculiar to individual churches, they painted diverse portraits of the New Testament's hero. But all of the gospel writers presented Jesus as a healer, a worker of wonders, a poetic preacher, one who had no truck with hypocrisy, and one especially concerned for the poor and the suffering. All also spoke of the opposition Jesus raised, of his call for faith, of his trust in his Father, and of the priority he gave to love. The evangelical Jesus is always in combat with Satan, under way toward the cross, and such a model of faith that his being raised by the Father is fitting. The Resurrection remains astounding, but it is a fitting consummation to Jesus' career.

The relation between Jesus and the Spirit has come in for much study recently,[3] and the upshot appears to be a greater appreciation that, from the outset of his career—indeed, from his conception—Jesus was formed and led by the Spirit. That relation only makes it the more fitting that Jesus resurrected would have sent the Spirit to the disciples to continue his mission with them. It only makes the love of God poured forth in our hearts by the Holy Spirit more clearly the grace of

Christ. Women who want to appreciate either the status of New Testament women or their own Christian status today have to get straight these New Testament assumptions. From experience, the Christians responsible for the New Testament were convinced that God had fulfilled the anticipations of Jeremiah and accomplished a new covenant, written on the heart by the Spirit.

> Behold, the days are coming, says the LORD, when I will make a new covenant with the house of Israel and the house of Judah, not like the covenant which I made with their fathers when I took them by the hand to bring them out of the land of Egypt, my covenant which they broke, though I was their husband, says the LORD. But this is the covenant which I will make with the house of Israel after those days, says the LORD: I will put my law within them, and I will write it upon their hearts; and I will be their God, and they shall be my people. And no longer shall each man teach his neighbor and each his brother, saying, "Know the LORD," for they shall all know me, from the least of them to the greatest, says the LORD; for I will forgive their iniquity, and I will remember their sin no more. (Jer. 31:31–34)

The early Christians, women as much as men, believed that the Spirit moving in their hearts was teaching them about God. They believed God had used Jesus to forgive sins and that the Spirit was testifying in their hearts that God was remembering their sins no more. Now they were children of God, members of God's family. Now the love of the Father for the Son, of the Son for the Father, and of the Father and Son both for the Spirit was circulating in their midst, in their hearts. They were to be a community of love, a signal to the outside world because of their love for one another. They were to abide in God's love, thinking the world a series of signs witnessing to that love's power and intimacy. While they lived, they were the Lord's. When they died, they were the

Lord's. So they ate the flesh of the Lord and drank his blood, in great gratitude. They entered the church by going down with Christ and rising, their baptism plunging them into the paschal mystery. The problem for their minds was how to manage such an embarrassment of riches, such significance and love flashing out at every angle. The problem for their hearts was to open wide enough to express their gratitude. With divine love at their founding and divine love at their goal, they were of all people the least to be pitied. With evil still flourishing in the world and the poor still legion, they were of all people the most puzzled. Women and men, they all looked to the Spirit to clarify what they needed to follow Christ. As we take up some New Testament texts about women, we must remember the primacy of the love of God that the early Christians assumed.

Discussion Questions

1. How does Jesus relate to the New Testament?
2. How was Jeremiah's new covenant associated with the Holy Spirit?
3. What in the love of God poured forth in the early Christians' hearts by the Holy Spirit was distinctly feminine?

Notes

1. Tikva Frymer-Kensky, "Women," in *HBD*, p. 1140.
2. See Elisabeth Schüssler-Fiorenza, *In Memory of Her* (New York: Crossroad, 1983).
3. See James D. G. Dunn, *Jesus and the Spirit* (Philadelphia: Westminster, 1975); Yves Congar, *I Believe in the Holy Spirit*, vol. 1 (New York: Crossroad, 1983).

13

Luke 1:30–31

And the angel said to her, "Do not be afraid, Mary, for you have found favor with God. And behold, you will conceive in your womb and bear a son, and you shall call his name Jesus."

A likely date for the Gospel of Luke is between 80 and 85 C.E. The majority of scholars now assume that Luke was not the companion of Paul on Paul's missionary journeys and that the two-volume work Luke-Acts is more theology than history. Like Paul, Luke is interested in the opening of the church to the Gentiles. His schema involves a threefold periodization of salvation history: the time of Israel, the time of Jesus, and the time of the church, when God's people became potentially worldwide. The majority opinion is that Luke was writing for a church with many Gentile converts. Among his distinctive themes are the responsibilities of the rich toward the poor and the significance of women. Luke probably composed his gospel from two major sources: Mark and the hypothetical Q (from *Quelle*, German for "source"). He may also have used materials peculiar to his own community. Overall, he has produced a gospel of high literary quality, to which we owe such memorable stories as the Good Samaritan and the Prodigal Son.

One of Luke's emphases is the providential plan of God. He sees what happened to Jesus, including his suffering and death, as decreed by a divine necessity. Thus the resurrected Christ says to the disconsolate disciples on the road to Emmaus, "O foolish men, and slow of heart to believe all that the prophets have spoken! Was it not necessary that the Christ should suffer these things and enter into his glory?" (24:25–26) No less providential was Mary's conception of Jesus, which inaugurated the middle phase of salvation history.

The angel speaking to Mary is Gabriel, known from the Book of Daniel (8:15–26; 9:21–27) as a messenger of God. His first words have told Mary that God is with her, but they have also disturbed her. So in our text Gabriel hastens to calm any fears. The favor Mary has found with God carries overtones of divine grace: God's blessing and life rest on her. The etymological thrust of the name *Jesus* is "Savior." The annunciation, as this scene traditionally is called, therefore concerns the birth of the one who will liberate Mary's people from their troubles, afflictions, and sins. Because Luke places Jesus' heredity in the line of Adam (3:38), the implication later becomes that Jesus is the Savior of the entire human race. When Mary asks how all this is to come to be, the angel promises an overshadowing by the Holy Spirit—conception by God's direct power. As a result, the child will be especially holy, a Son of God.

All this comes to pass, and thereby Mary becomes the first lady of Christian history. The basis for all her titles and the veneration accorded her down through the ages was her being the mother of Jesus. Indeed, because Jesus was believed divine, Mary's most important title was Theotokos: the one who bore God. From her, divinity had taken flesh, so that it could dwell among us. She was the link, the nexus, between the power of the Most High and the flesh passed down from Adam and Eve. The incarnation of the Logos depended on her cooperation. Thus Mary's response to the angel became a paradigm of religious obedience: "Behold, I am the handmaid of the Lord; let it be to me according to your word" (Luke 1:38). She was the perfect instrument, the acceptable and accepting vehicle, the great yea-sayer. Even though medieval Christian piety often stressed Mary's sufferings at the cross, Christian art as a whole has placed more emphasis on the divine maternity: the annunciation, the Madonna and child. Usually the Madonna is serene, the baby angelic. Often there are overtones of the sufferings to come, but perhaps as frequently there is a reginal accent: she is the Queen of Heaven, because her son is the savior-king.

Mary's other appearances in the Gospels place her among the disciples of Jesus and stress that she had to struggle to understand what her son was up to. Thus after worrying that he was lost and finding him in the temple discoursing with the teachers, she had to ponder what he meant by saying that of course he would be in his father's house (Luke 2:49–51). She occasioned the sign Jesus gave at Cana of Galilee, when he turned the water into wine (John 2:1–11), and her presence at the cross marked her as faithful to the bitter end. Such privileges as her Immaculate Conception (being conceived without sin) and her assumption into heaven were inferred from her dignity as the mother of God.

As the foremost New Testament woman, Mary understandably became the model of feminine Christian piety. Virgin and mother, Lady of Sorrows and Queen of Heaven, she offered a wide range of wonders to contemplate and virtues to imitate. Perhaps the two most influential in Christian piety were her virginal purity and her maternal love. Both are provocative nowadays, as Christian feminists try to work out a spirituality suitable for present, liberated times.

Whether or not one accepts the full-blown version of Mary's virginity, which has included virginal birth and living with Joseph as sister and brother, one ought to ponder the purity implied in the scene of the annunciation. Mary is presented as a young girl, perhaps barely beyond puberty. Women usually married young in Jesus' time, and they were expected to come to marriage as virgins. This standard did not have to mean prudishness or ignorance of family life. It is unlikely in Mary's case that it meant much shelter from domestic work or witnessing women's lot. The purity implied by the text also was not "spiritual," as many periods of Christian piety tended to assume. It had no bias against the body. Judaism in Mary's time was holistic, as we see in the epistles of Paul. "Spirit" usually meant the whole person in its upward, God-directed aspects. The purity at issue here was that befitting the conception of God's child. Because Jesus was to be the Savior, the foremost holy man, it was fitting that his mother should have found favor with God, should have been pure and good. We should think of young girls who are innocent but not naive, of older women (religious, single or married) who shine with integrity. At its best, the cult of the Virgin reminded women and men of beauty of spirit—what happens in genuine holiness. At its worst, it helped people despise the flesh and feel that holiness was either beyond them or so inhuman it was despicable.

As the Blessed Mother, Mary was preeminently the woman most identified with Jesus' mission and most wounded by his crucifixion. Extrapolating from what it took to be natural maternal emotions, traditional piety elaborated the piercing of Mary's soul (Luke 2:35) predicted at Jesus' presentation to the Lord and fulfilled at the cross. It also puzzled about New Testament passages where Jesus seemed harsh to Mary and subordinated parent-child relations to the demands of discipleship (John 2:4; Matt. 12:46–50). Whatever Mary's maternal joys, Marian piety tended to stress her sorrows. She was the Sorrowful Mother, a queen whose crown shared the thorns of Jesus' own.

An impressive number of women identified with Mary's suffering motherhood. Just as ordinary people found the suffering Christ approachable because, like them, he was in pain, so ordinary people, men as well as women, found the suffering Mary approachable. She too knew the price faith could exact. She too had been tried and put to the test. If the Blessed Virgin could seem remote, an ideal only glimpsed from afar, the Sorrowful Mother seemed like one of their own. She would intercede with her son, and he would deny her nothing. Did not most mothers, whether queens or peasants, hope as much? Did not patriarchal society teach them to glory in raising sons and expect that their lot would improve in the measure their sons prospered? The peculiar twist in the case of Mary was her altruism, which matched that of her son. As he had not sought his own glory but that of his heavenly Father, so she would not use his success for her own sake but to benefit those petitioning his favor.

To rehabilitate Mary as a model for Christian feminists, one has both to stress the strength implied in her vocation and underscore her identification with the poor. Taking the latter first, one might emphasize the Magnificat (Luke 1:47–55), where Hannah's song is reworked in view of Mary's appreciation of the new phase of salvation history in which she has become involved. For instance, "He has scattered the proud in the imagination of their hearts, he has put down the mighty from their thrones, and exalted those of low degree; he has filled the hungry with good things, and the rich he has sent empty away" (vv. 51–53). Insofar as Mary is identified with the poor and the hungry, she becomes the mother of people yearning for liberation everywhere, especially in the third world. No wonder she means so much in Latin American Catholicism.

Mary developed and exercised her strength, to be sure, within the confining roles available to her in the patriarchal society of her day. But such strength was no less real, as it has been no less real in strong daughters, wives, and mothers the patriarchal world over. We do not have to approve such patriarchal limitations to admire Mary's strength. We need only realize how much mettle always comes out through suffering, keeping faith, doing what one can do in imperfect circumstances. Women above all ought to know that principle, so women above all ought to be able to call Mary sister and friend.[1]

Discussion Questions

1. Why does the angel bid Mary not to be afraid?
2. What symbolic value does Mary's purity retain?
3. How does Mary relate to liberation theology?

Note

1. For stimulating reflection on New Testament women in general and Mary in particular, see Rosemary Haughton, *The Re-Creation of Eve* (Springfield, Ill.: Templegate, 1985).

14

Mark 14:6

But Jesus said, "Let her alone; why do you trouble her? She has done a beautiful thing to me."

The majority of New Testament scholars consider Mark the oldest of the Gospels, probably written shortly after the fall of Jerusalem to Roman soldiers in 70 C.E. It seems to have come from a church outside of Palestine and to have been written for people who did not understand Aramaic, the language that predominated in Palestine in the first century C.E. Among the theological motifs prominent in Mark, perhaps the strongest is its concentration on suffering. Jesus above all is the Messiah who had to suffer misunderstanding, conflict, and a painful death. Christian disciples therefore ought to plan on misunderstanding, conflict, and even a painful death. The disciple is not greater or different than the Master, when it comes to the clash between faith and worldly, unconverted values. Those who think Jesus should have come in pomp and wielded worldly, even military, power are badly mistaken. Like the disciples who fled when Jesus was arrested, they have not understood the heart of the gospel, its overturning of common sense and carnal values. Jesus was in combat with Satan. His healing and exorcisms represented the power of heaven tri-

umphing over the power of ungodliness. The writer of Mark
expected Jesus to return soon to complete his triumph. The
Resurrection was but the down payment on the full redemption of humanity from Satan's thrall.

Our text occurs near the end of Mark, when Jesus has
entered upon his final week in Jerusalem. Jesus has taught in
the temple and uttered the apocalyptic sayings we find in
Mark 13. Everything is building toward the climax of Mark's
dramatic scenario when the Roman centurion declares, "Truly
this man was the Son of God" (15:39). From the outset (1:1),
Mark has promised good news about Jesus Christ the Son of
God, but much of the time Jesus has shrouded his identity in
secrecy. As he approaches the passion, however, the need for
secrecy falls away. The chief priests and scribes are plotting to
kill him. So at a dinner party close to Passover, Jesus lets an
unnamed woman anoint him, as a prefiguration of his burial.
The party takes place in the home of Simon the leper, a man
with whom a rabbi concerned about strict interpretation of
the laws of cleanliness would not have associated. Some of the
disciples are indignant that Jesus lets the woman perform such
a wasteful act (the ointment was expensive). They think the
money should have been given to the poor. Our text is the first
lines of Jesus' reply. Only Jesus sees the beauty of what the
woman has done. Only Jesus defends her.

Let us deal first with Jesus' defense and then with the
beauty of the woman's act. Imagination paints a scene of
several men blustering about what the woman has done,
arguing its merits and demerits. The disciples, like many
other religious groups, did not lack for people too free with
their opinions. In Mark 8, when Jesus predicts his death,
Peter upbraids him. Jesus then has to rebuke Peter, telling
him that he thinks more like Satan than like God. Something
of that rebuke carries over here. Although they are at the
verge of Jesus' passion, the disciples still do not understand.
Indeed, they will abandon Jesus, while a handful of women

will keep faith. The implication is that the unnamed woman acted from the heart, feeling that Jesus had come into crisis. The blustery disciples were debating on the level of principles: should not extra money be given to the poor? They were some of the first Christian puritans, oblivious to feelings and beauty.

In defending the woman, Jesus speaks up for people of good heart who often are bullied by loudmouths and those of strong opinion. Most patriarchal cultures would stereotype women as meeker and more emotional, men as more likely to debate about principles. Here the point probably is not that Jesus needed the ointment or sought the attention the woman's act produced. The point is that the woman was being criticized by people who had missed the meaning of her action and were presuming to an authority they did not possess. As Jesus generally championed the poor, so here he champions the one needing defense. The loudmouths can take care of themselves. A woman probably astounded to find herself the center of attention, confused that her spontaneous act should have been subjected to critical analysis, needs protection and encouragement. What she has done is close to the kingdom of God. Jesus is bound to defend her and to silence her critics.

Concerning the beauty of the woman's action, we must pause a little longer. The very next verse is extremely provocative: "For you always have the poor with you, and whenever you will, you can do good to them; but you will not always have me." Is the implication that the critics are hypocritical? Is this speaking up for the poor a new note, something that hitherto they have hardly made a daily affair? Jesus does not denigrate good works or generosity toward the poor. He is irritated by the speciousness of using generosity toward the poor as a club to brutalize a good deed sprung from a good heart. As well, he is saddened that the woman has grasped the sense of the occasion, the nearness of his end, while the more prominent disciples have not. She has sensed what is fitting, while they have blundered along as usual. Jesus finds important not abstract principles but sensitivity to concrete and present realities. People who cannot feel the finger of God in existential situations are bound to misconstrue them. People who live amid abstract principles rather than flesh-and-blood sisters and brothers are always going to be a problem. When they hold religious authority, they become an outright menace.

Perhaps this is the place to speak up for the rights of several aspects of religious discipleship often associated with women. They include sensitivity, love of beauty, emotion, alertness to details, shyness, and intuition. There are other places where it is appropriate to defend the rights of reason, the usefulness of skepticism and hardheadedness. For every virtue there is a time, and for every gift a purpose under heaven. But here we ought to celebrate and promote the gifts of feeling. The woman was moved by Jesus, by his beauty and pathos. She wanted to do something, to make a gesture, to offer love, respect, and consolation. So she did. We do not know whether the ointment took all her money or was something she could easily afford. Neither do we know whether she regularly helped the poor or had little awareness of them. All we know is that what she did pleased Jesus, appealed to his sense of what was fitting. If only because it served as a good vehicle for the woman's faith and love, it was a fine, sacramental action. When the disciples criticized it, it became all the more impressive: the dullards again had missed the point, misunderstanding both the woman's intention and the significance of the moment. So Jesus rather roughly reprimanded them. Beauty had its own rights. Sensitive understanding ought not to be deprecated.

One of the blind spots to which some of the best religious people and most generous activists are prone keeps them from appreciating the beauty of God. Religion without steady work for social justice certainly is suspect, but religion that has little concern for beauty easily becomes stiff and dutiful. As well, beauty keeps religion from the earnestness that soon grows oppressive and sometimes leads people to kick over the traces. Song, dance, religious art, poetry—these are not luxuries but essentials. Unless we warm to God, weep tears of gratitude and sadness both, feel stirred in mind, heart, soul, and loins, we do not give God the return the divine warmth deserves.

Astonishingly, God finds human beings beautiful. There are things we can do, things we are, profiles we show, that touch God's heart. God is in love with us and our world. Grace comes with a glow. Even when God is suffering our stupidities and sins, a beautiful act affords a pause that refreshes. One of the best results of the church's movement into a multicultural, truly global world is the boost it can give our appreciation of human beauty. Christ is lovelier in limbs and faces nowaways, because they are more colorful. And many of the cultures gaining new importance in the church value emotion, feeling, soul more than European and North American cultures have. Many insist that praise of God rise up joyously, with sounds of drums, with garments of brilliant hue. I see the small, frightened woman who anointed Jesus' head as a mother of this latter-day affirmation of beauty. I see her as a permanent rebuke to the grim, dutiful, overly principled types who have more words than feelings. Again and again they have the experience but miss the appropriate feeling. Again and again they undervalue the beauty of the Lord.

Discussion Questions

1. Why does the Gospel of Mark stress Jesus' sufferings?
2. Does this gospel scene justify letting the poor take care of themselves?
3. What is the beauty in the woman's action, and how relevant is it to religion as a whole?

15

Matthew 27:55

There were also many women there, looking on from afar, who had followed Jesus from Galilee, ministering to him.

Like Luke, Matthew apparently was written (or edited into final form) about 85 C.E. and drew upon both Mark and Q, as well as traditions peculiar to its own community. This gospel likely came from a predominantly Jewish Christian community, perhaps one located in Antioch, and one of its major concerns was to show how Jesus had fulfilled the expectations associated with the Messiah. Jesus appears as the giver of a new Torah, as a new Moses. The Matthean community manifestly was hostile to Jews who had not accepted Jesus as the Messiah, and the conflicts between Jews and Christians after the fall of Jerusalem in 70 C.E., which led to Christians' being expelled from the synagogue, are the best explanation for such hostility.

Our text occurs towards the end of the gospel, when Jesus has been nailed to the cross and has died. According to Matthew this event occasioned the tearing of the curtain of the temple in two and an earthquake that opened the tombs of many holy people. Matthew repeats Mark's usage in having the Roman centurion confess that Jesus truly was the Son of God, although for Matthew the earthquake seems to have been the stimulus to confess, whereas for Mark the manner of Jesus' death sufficed.

Our text comes after the centurion's confession, like a documentary afterthought. Following it are the names of some of the female disciples: Mary Magdalene, Mary the mother of James and Joseph, and the mother of the sons of Zebedee. They are entered on the historical record as eyewitnesses. Mary Magdalene will have special status as the first witness of the Resurrection and the one who brings the news to the inner circle of Jesus' disciples. But here the author of Matthew is buttressing the historicity of his account by claiming that certain specific people were witnesses. Obliquely, perhaps without intending it, he (all probability is that the Gospels were written by men, although we cannot be certain) opens a window onto the early Christian community, reminding us that women had followed Jesus from the beginning and that some were faithful to the bitter end.

The phrase "looking on from afar" strikes me as especially poignant, because it has fitted so many historical situations. Regularly throughout patriarchal history, women have been bystanders, onlookers, people witnessing from the margins. As with this gospel, no one asks them what they think, what they feel, how the event is changing their lives. The implication here is that they cared enough about Jesus to stick by him to the end. It was not healthy to be associated with Jesus, after the religious and political establishments had declared him persona non grata. It could only have hurt one's reputation, social standing, and pocketbook. The women seem not to have cared. He had touched their hearts, perhaps touched their limbs and cured them. He had spoken of a kingdom in which people such as themselves, people of little account in their society, would have equal status under God. Indeed, he had challenged the prevailing legalism and misogynism, which had twisted their lives. So they could no more abandon him than they could abandon their selves. He had become the treasure of those selves, the meaning of their lives. They would not let him die alone. Painful as it was, they would not deprive themselves of a last glimpse of him.

In the last reflection, we considered a woman who acted from the heart and did a beautiful thing to Jesus. In this reflection, we deal with a tableau, a familiar scene, the prelude to the Pietà, when the mother of Jesus, one of the last onlookers, takes the dead body in her arms. Both cases focus our attention on something simple and whole. Both provide matter more for simple contemplation than for intellectual analysis. Depending on how an artist painted the women's faces, arranged their limbs, and set their posture, we would sense more or less pain, would feel more or less despair. But every sympathetic instinct inclines one to dismiss curiosity or masochism. Every assumption of basic health on the women's part inclines one to suspect profound grief without making it the center of the women's experience. For grief stresses one's own loss, while the women are better remembered as having mainly wished to console Jesus, help him feel less abandoned, and condole with his mother.

All of this is imaginative reconstruction, of course, and one does not know how pious to make it. There was nothing pious about the nails, the thirst, and the death. The disappointment and shame, too, were brutally real. Yet, the women stayed, while most of the men fled. The women were better equipped for the harsh reality. Perhaps, in the men's defense, we should note that the women were less likely to be judged conspirators of Jesus and similarly dangerous to the public security. Perhaps the women were culturally better prepared for emotional losses and burying the dead. But it remains intriguing that the women stayed, endured, and did not leave until the last act. It remains provocative: is religious discipleship stereotypically feminine in its gambling everything on love?

Such a question is dangerous nowadays, and I will not answer it. It probes and prods simply by being asked, however, because it focuses discipleship on an affective gamble obviously best assimilated to a love affair. Such a love affair certainly is not the exclusive prerogative of women. Neither is it limited to sexual passion between adults. A parent can love a child with a hunger, an irrationality, that goes to the same crux. A friend can feel for a friend so strongly that rational considerations are secondary. In the best cases, of course, reason is not ousted but sublated: taken up to a higher level, set in a bigger and better context. Overall, reason both justifies and is justified by passionate religious love: giving one's heart to the divine beauty, falling head over heels for the divine mystery, is the most reasonable thing one can do. But on the everyday level, where mystical insight often does not rule, discipleship like that of the women looking on Jesus crucified makes most sense as a religious passion, an obsession and commitment like that of a lover taken out of herself by the treasure on which her heart has fixed.

When the biblical God had to be fitted to Greek philosophical categories, it seemed clear that divinity could not change or suffer. Jesus obviously had suffered in his humanity, and that humanity was united to the divine Logos, so by accommodation (*communicatio idiomatum*) one could say that the Logos had suffered and died. Still, orthodox Christian theology struggled to find ways of involving God with the world and explaining redemption as God's love affair with creation. We still lack a metaphysics capable of handling these problems, and I myself do not think process theology will supply it, because I find process theology insufficiently awed by either the divine transcendence (the complete self-sufficiency of God) or the sharp, angular, highly individualistic humanity of Jesus. Nonetheless, the best gropings after understanding of how God suffers in, with, and for our world undoubtedly stem from appreciations of passionate love. The women standing by Jesus suffered in the measure they loved. Because they loved, they shielded themselves less than those who could not take it and had to flee. It was more important to accompany Jesus, give him what support they could, than to bandage their own souls. They had no choice, could do no other. Any special strength or grace involved welled up without their thinking about it. The Spirit who sustained Jesus sustained them, because the bond between them and Jesus was the primordial tie of love.

Love is so primitive a term, so basic and constitutive an emotion, that we seldom illumine it very well. It rather illumines everything else, from education to art, from healing to creativity. Creative science comes from the love of understanding, the absorption with the physical world. Creative parenting comes from having one's heart stolen away, wanting to eat the little beauty up and die rather than hurt her or his soul. The church flourishes in the measure its leaders and common folk love the humanity possible in the freedom for which Christ has set Christians free. The dead ends of warfare, interpersonal hatred, economic injustice, racial prejudice, and a dozen other social disorders seem to yield only when a prophet like Gandhi or Martin Luther King, Jr., looks upon the antagonists with profound love. Such love simply is beyond us, most of the time. We generally lack the capacity to be human as we want to be. Without the Spirit of God breathing in us, vivifying our souls, we just do not have the being, just are not good enough, to do what has to be done. But occasionally, one of our kind, a limited creature recognizably like ourselves, is borne by the Spirit to achieve the otherwise impossible. Occasionally men like Gandhi and King climb the mountaintop, women like those who stayed by the cross accomplish the one thing necessary. And because they do, occasionally we remember that love is strong as death, that God is deathless love.

Discussion Questions

1. What has centuries of "looking on from afar" taught women?
2. What are the problems with conceiving discipleship as a love affair?
3. How is the divine Spirit involved in the reasons of the heart?

16

John 4:39

Many Samaritans from that city believed in him be-
cause of the woman's testimony, "He told me all that I
ever did."

If the Synoptic Gospels constitute a first major bloc of New
Testament materials, the Johannine literature (gospel, epistles, Revelation) constitutes a second. Most New Testament
scholars think this literature arose a decade or so later than
Luke and Matthew, perhaps from a church centered in
Ephesus. The Johannine communities apparently struggled
over the issue of Jesus' divinity, which brought concomitant
debates over Jesus' humanity. Raymond Brown has offered a
hypothesis that fits the complicated data.[1] The legacy bequeathed the church catholic by the Johannine literature includes a "high" Christology (one stressing the divinity of the
Logos), a profound appreciation of incarnation and so sacra-
mentality, and an insistence on the inner gifts of the Holy
Spirit. The authority behind John, described as the "beloved
disciple," apparently was stimulated by Hellenistic thought
and sought to unify a world of spirit with a world of embodi-
ment. Thus we find the first part of the gospel structured by
seven "signs" Jesus works—seven manifestations of the light,
life, and love the Father sent the Son to reveal.

Our text comes at the conclusion of an episode in which Jesus discourses with a Samaritan woman. Rabbis of his day by choice had little to do with women, and Samaritans were considered heretics to stay away from. Simply by interacting with the woman, Jesus thus amazed his disciples. Moreover, the interaction gave the author of John the occasion for Jesus' discourse on living water (faith, signed by baptism) that wells up into eternal life. As in many Johannine exchanges, irony pervades. The woman either misunderstands or pretends to take Jesus literally, for they are at a well. Jesus is speaking of spiritual reality, and she is interested in easing her work load: "Sir, give me this water, that I may not thirst, nor come here to draw" (4:15).

Jesus then delves into the matter of her marital life, which to say the least, has been messy. Wanting to get away from that topic, the woman asks him about the dispute between the Jews and the Samaritans. Jesus gives the orthodox answer favoring Jewish traditions but places the whole dispute in a new setting: the time is coming when questions such as where to worship God will be irrelevant because it will be clear that God, the Father, can and must be worshiped everywhere, in spirit and truth. This reply so impresses the woman that she is sure Jesus is the Messiah whom Jews and Samaritans alike have been awaiting. Eventually, by processes we are not shown, the woman gets many of her neighbors to meet Jesus and come around to her high estimate of him. Thus our text: many believed because of the woman's testimony, which was rooted in Jesus' understanding of her life.

It would be easy to develop the implications of the freedom with which Jesus dealt with the Samaritan woman, but that freedom may be fairly well known.[2] Just as Jesus felt free to consort with those considered "sinners"—prostitutes, tax collectors—so he felt free to heal on the Sabbath and interact with women. Without despising the customs of his people, Jesus subordinated them to what he considered the imperative needs of his mission or the requirements of the people he was encountering. In this case, circumstances had set him in contact with a Samaritan woman. Why, then, not use the occasion to extend his mission to her? Why not, in the process, break the stereotypes that prejudice had erected between Jews and Samaritans and drive home the point that a new era was dawning when all such antagonisms would be revealed as passé?

The Gospel of John regularly associates Jesus' signs with faith and makes them evidence that Jesus should have been accepted by his people as the Messiah. Like Matthew, John is bitter that the Jews largely rejected Jesus, so his portraits of the Jews are slanted against them. Here the Samaritan woman serves much as the Roman centurion served at the end of Mark and Matthew. She is a witness from outside the mainstream of Jesus' own people who was able to see what for John was obvious: the wisdom and power of Jesus had accredited him as the Messiah.

Did Jesus read the woman's mind? Who knows. Perhaps something in the woman's bearing suggested she was loose about marital fidelity. Probably she was interesting on other grounds, however, for Jesus treats her as a person who could be lured by metaphors. She was willing to puzzle over his statement about living water. She reasoned that this maker of riddles, this seer into emotions, might have an interesting opinion about the religious differences between Samaritans and Jews, so she put him a question. And all he had to do to get her very interested was to tell her what he knew, share his convictions. This openness brought her to make a confession of her own: she was awaiting the Messiah. Jesus then said to her, "I who speak to you am he"—a clarity of self-revelation hard to find in the Synoptics.

Apparently convinced, the woman hurried off to share her experience (probably partly to brag, partly to let others in on the coming of the Messiah). She acted on her experience, did something about her new insight and faith. The Johannine literature is keenly aware that faith—inmost conviction—has to be enacted. The liberation theologian José Miranda has seized on this Johannine awareness as a key to the theology that might free people of their oppressions.[3] So the woman stands as a model listener, an interlocutor after Jesus' own heart. She was struck, dealt honestly with what she found, took it to heart, and acted upon it. In her the sower found good ground and so bountiful yield.

Today many theologians are interested in narrative or story. Thinking hard about both the form in which biblical revelation has been cast and the way that people tend to clarify their personal identity, theologians are realizing that at the center of faith stands the script God and we are writing. In this context, the woman's words "He told me all that I ever did" strike a responsive chord. Jesus had clarified the woman's life story. He had helped her structure her time, see where she had been and where she could be going. And though the woman may initially have been struck by his insight into her having been much married, it seems likely she soon became more interested in salvation: where to find the Messiah. Jesus was offering her a new interpretation of her possibilities. She need not think of herself as a being condemned to haul water and pleasure men. She could be a witness to salvation, a sharer and proclaimer of great good news. In offering her this new set of possibilities, this fresh way of defining herself, Jesus was gambling that she had the wherewithal to catch his drift, the gumption to make a change. He was not disappointed. The woman is in the Gospel of John not simply to occasion a couple of speeches about water, food, and messiahship. She is in the gospel as a model of faith.

Interestingly, Jesus paid the woman's past little heed. Although she had been married five times (whether because of forces beyond her control or because of her own inclinations), she stood before him as a new candidate, a free agent. The past had not foreclosed her chance to enter the Kingdom of God. Because of her own character (she had learned enough from the past to pay attention to Jesus and notice his special gifts) and Jesus' vote of confidence in her, the woman could be turned around. Conversion can be as simple as she demonstrated: honesty about where one is and willingness to follow a more excellent way.

On the evidence of this episode, God is not a moralist, sticking people in boxes according to their past behavior. People can come alive, feel the stirrings of grace, if they meet someone willing to engage them directly. Jesus treated the woman as intelligent. He paid her the honor of assuming she could catch his drift. The more she pressed, the more forthcoming he was, until she wrung from him the declaration of his messiahship. In this light, the woman seems not just honest and decisive but also shrewd. Using a typically feminine interest in people and skill at drawing them out, she got Jesus to reveal more of himself than he may initially have intended. On the other hand, she got herself more deeply involved than she may initially have intended, but to her credit she saw the matter through. So I think of her as an object lesson in what might happen anytime we take other people seriously and speak to them about matters of real moment. I think of her as a witness credible because she opened her heart and let God reveal how he would have her cleanse and deepen her love.

Discussion Questions

1. What are the main implications of the traditional tendency of holy men to avoid contacts with women?
2. How does the Samaritan woman exemplify conversion and discipleship?
3. Why is faith so frequently a story of transforming people's love?

Notes

1. Raymond E. Brown, *The Community of the Beloved Disciple* (New York: Paulist, 1979); see also John Carmody, Denise Lardner Carmody, and Gregory A. Robbins, *Exploring the New Testament* (Englewood Cliffs, N.J.: Prentice-Hall, 1986), pp. 265–309.

2. See Ben Witherington III, *Women in the Ministry of Jesus* (Cambridge: Cambridge University Press, 1984).

3. José Miranda, *Being and the Messiah* (Maryknoll, N.Y.: Orbis, 1976).

17

John 11:5

Now Jesus loved Martha and her sister and Lazarus.

The raising of Lazarus from the dead is the seventh and greatest of the signs the Johannine Jesus works in the first half of the gospel. At the outset of this story, we learn that Lazarus was ill in Bethany and that he was the brother of Mary, the woman who anointed the Lord with ointment and wiped his feet (see John 12:1–3). Whether that action was the same as the anointing we have seen in Matthew is unclear. For our purposes, it does not matter. I am more interested in the statement that Jesus loved this family of two sisters and a brother. The remainder of the story proves this love, explicitly so at 11:36, where Jesus weeps over the dead Lazarus and the onlookers say, "See how he loved him!" Certainly the bearing of Martha and Mary toward Jesus is one of great respect. They call him Lord and profess faith that he is the Messiah. But none of this formality detracts from the emotional bonds among the four. When Mary weeps for her dead brother, Jesus is moved both to tears and to action.

We see, then, that Jesus not only interacted with women freely but shared strong ties. Women such as Martha and Mary could be his friends, people he cared deeply about.

Without overthrowing the customs of his day, Jesus took away much of their misogynistic sting. Anyone thinking about Jesus' love for Martha and Mary would be hard pressed to justify discrimination against women. Anyone claiming that women were unfit for ministry in the church or leadership in society would have to contend with women's manifest fitness for friendship with the Lord. If Martha and Mary could be intimate with the head of the church, could serve the Son of God, how could women be unsuited for ministries based on holiness or leadership aiming at serving people Jesus had served? The women we contemplated standing by Jesus at the cross had ministered to him throughout his public life. The women we contemplate here were not only believers, they were people Jesus liked to be with, people whose sufferings Jesus shared and whose joys he sought to augment.

When we consider the heart of the Christian message, we inevitably find ourselves dealing with love. All of our analogies for God's love come into play, especially parenting and marriage. Friendship is another important analogy, and here we find it in sharp focus. Despite the exalted status and honor he bore as leader of a new religious movement, Jesus had time for friends. Indeed, when one considers his attending weddings and parties and his opponents' criticism that he was a glutton and drunkard (Matt. 11:19; Luke 7:34), it becomes plausible that his preferred form of discipleship was friendship. Any doubts about this possibility vanish in the second half of John's gospel, when signs give way to the manifestation of Jesus' glory. In the midst of his high-priestly prayer, when he is speaking as much to the Father as to the disciples, the Johannine Jesus asserts: "No longer do I call you servants, for the servant does not know what his master is doing; but I have called you friends, for all that I have heard from my Father I have made known to you" (John 15:15). What does this statement suggest for feminist religion?

First, it suggests that women, as well as men, have alternatives to the religious paradigms of servant and master, follower and lord, child and parent, wife and husband. They can think of God or Jesus as their friend. This conception does not rule out their also thinking of God or Jesus as their lover. Just as the same human person can be both lover and friend (as the best marriages show), so the same divinity can be both the focus of one's deepest romance and the closest sharer of the thoughts in one's heart. However, the largely hierarchical and masculine imagery in which Western divinity has been cast has obscured the possibilities of women's friendship with God. Men, feeling awkward about nuptial imagery for God, often have gravitated toward companionship, collaboration, and friendship. The nuptial imagery has been easier for women, but somewhat detrimental to women's enjoyment of God as a friend. Martha and Mary were privileged to enjoy Jesus as their friend, and the obvious warmth of that relationship may help today's religious women realize that friendship need not be the taciturn, apparently undemonstrative relationship it seems to be for many men. It can be warm and full of heart.

As such, friendship may serve well the women who want to explore the feminine dimensions of the Godhead but who do not find motherhood a fully satisfying analogy. Motherhood certainly can serve our approaches to God very well, as fatherhood can, but women seeking not just more of their own gender in God but also more affirmation of their autonomy can find motherhood problematic. This is not to say that mothers cannot affirm the adulthood of their children. It is simply to grope after a companionship with God, a sharing of life, less freighted with parent-child emotions and more useful for collaboration and socializing. The women at the cross had ministered to Jesus serving him as he worked for others. Martha and Mary knew Jesus as a welcome guest in their home, a regular at their parties and times of sorrowing. Any relationships or symbols that open our hearts and make us cleave to God are blessed. Friendship can accomplish such opening, so friendship with God, collaboration and socializing with Jesus, can be blessed.

It is rather speculative to imagine precisely feminist friendship with either Jesus or the divine mystery in its feminine aspects, but perhaps worth trying. How do mature women nowadays carry out honest friendships with men? How do they carry out honest friendships with fellow women?

Any friendship naturally occurs not in the abstract but between two specific people—indeed, between two people who usually share other acquaintances and so have for one another a persona shaped by much more than their own one-to-one interactions. Thus Mary and John can be friends because they get on well at work, or because they are part of a group that meets twice a month for bowling and beer, or because one is the friend of the spouse of the other. They will not be significant friends, however, unless a spark occurs peculiar to themselves. It is a nice task to determine what in such a spark comes from eros, the force of attraction toward the beautiful or the good, and what comes from philia, the force of like-mindedness, of being sympatico. Fortunately, we need not trouble about that distinction here. If our friendship with God is both erotic and based in like-mindedness, so much the better. If our friendship with a person of the opposite sex blends the two, fine—as long as we honor our other commitments. The more important point is what the attraction enables: revelation, communication, and sharing. Friendship, like romantic love, frees us to show and be more of who we are, more of the self we feel tender toward and worry about. It enables us to speak with another out of a pledge, usually more unspoken than verbalized, that we like one another, cherish one another, think one another wonderful. So we can both kid around and console one another. We can both play and kiss away the tears.

We do not see much of Jesus' play with Martha and Mary,

but we do see his comforting them. Minimal as it may seem, the women at the cross were comforting Jesus—as friends standing by, doing the best they could. So there was some reciprocity in women's friendships with Jesus. There were things given as well as things received. The marvel about friendship in particular and the human condition in general is that there always can be. The benefactor needs people to receive the benefaction. The teacher needs the student. And the more we reflect on these relationships in the horizon of heaven, the less the disparity between the two partners seems to be. With due changes, we can apply this kind of relationship to God. Having chosen to create the world and incarnate the Son, God has established relationships in which God receives as well as gives.

The benefits of heterosexual friendship include further mutual instruction in the fullness of human nature. Through the differences, complementarities, and oppositions we experience, we realize "human nature" is rich beyond comprehension. Friendship with God might bring analogous realizations about the permutations of the divine-human relationship. God as masculine friend, as well as father, brother, and spouse, is God dealing with a woman out of an intriguing otherness. Conversely, God as feminine friend, as well as mother and sister, is God dealing with a woman out of an intriguing sameness. The like-mindedness of two female friends, the things they can easily understand, assume, and share, makes life easier and richer. Why should not dealing with God as a female companion make religious life the same?

Because of the historical association between divinity and masculinity in the West (in the East, divinity is bisexual), women have not had much stimulus to treat God as their sister or female friend (the motherhood of God has been stronger).[1] The Virgin Mary certainly has supplied much of the symbolism women have needed,[2] but nothing in Christian theology determines that God could not be approached as a female friend. The limits of our approaches to God stem less from orthodoxy than from our imaginations. Whatever is noble and compatible with such divine attributes as mystery, infinity, and love can serve as an analogy taking us to God. As men may in the future develop Christian nuptial symbolism to picture the religious life as romancing a feminine God, so women certainly may develop figures for sisterhood and female friendship with a divinity they project through their womanhood.

Discussion Questions

1. Create a script for a brief, happy interaction between Jesus and his friends Martha and Mary.

2. What are the implications of women's responding to Jesus as a friend?

3. What are the implications of women's responding to God as a sister or female friend?

Notes

1. See Carolyn Walker Bynum, *Jesus as Mother* (Berkeley: University of California Press, 1982).

2. See Marina Warner, *Alone of All Her Sex: The Myth and Cult of the Virgin Mary* (New York: Knopf, 1976).

18

John 20:18

Mary Magdalene went and said to the disciples, "I have seen the Lord"; and she told them that he had said these things to her.

The scene is the commission by the Johannine risen Christ that makes Mary Magdalene his apostle to the apostles. Peter and the disciple whom Jesus loved have run to the tomb because Mary has visited it and found the stone taken away. They have seen the linen cloths in which Jesus had been wrapped but, finding the tomb empty, have returned to their homes. Mary has lingered, unable to leave the spot last inhabited by her beloved Lord. She is weeping and confused. Two angels inquire about her weeping, and then a voice turns her around. It is Jesus, although she does not recognize him. Only when he calls her by name does she realize it is her Teacher. Jesus tells her not to embrace him because he has yet to ascend to the Father. Then he gives her the charge to tell his brethren that he is ascending to his Father and their Father, to his God and their God. Our verse reports that Mary carries out her commission.

The Magdalene has been a favorite subject of Christian art, often in juxtaposition to Mary the mother of Jesus.[1] If Mary the mother of Jesus could represent purity and maternal emotion, the Magdalene could represent passionate involvement with the man Jesus. Tradition made her a sinner out of whom Jesus had cast seven devils (Mark 16:9). Usually the assumption was that her failings had included sexual sins, if not prostitution. Love of Jesus had given all her passion a new, pure focus. So artists portrayed her with flaming red hair, clinging to the feet of Jesus or devastated at the cross. A wildness, an emotional excess considered unseemly for the Virgin, completely fitted the Magdalene. And because God had forgiven her much, she loved to exceptional measure. Indeed, God had made her one of the greatest saints, the one privileged to see the victorious Jesus first and announce the glad tidings of the Resurrection.

Pious Christian speculation often filled out the biblical accounts of the Resurrection by assuring that the resurrected Christ first appeared to his mother. The argument here was from what was fitting, as have been the arguments for the Virgin's Immaculate Conception and her assumption into heaven. But if one sticks to the letter of the New Testament text, Mary Magdalene is the one who first experienced the fact of the Resurrection, the reality of Jesus' triumph. It is intriguing to link this privilege with the character ascribed to the Magdalene in the Gospels.

The most obvious inference is that Mary Magdalene was at the tomb and was privileged to see Jesus because, of all the disciples, she most could not bear, would not accept, the departure of her Lord. It is almost as though her desire and need for him were so great that he had to appear. And this line of reflection points up the possibility that faith, hope, and love, the inseparable triad of theological virtues, can become so intense an identification with God that one insists God must live—holy love must be not just the best possibility we can find in our world but our world's very cause and foundation. Far from being just a pale possibility, let alone a chimera, the divine love would then be the realest thing there is. From the outset, it would explain our existence and nature—why we are and how we have been made. To be sure, this line of thought is a rather metaphysical extrapolation from a simple gospel scene. Mary's seeking Jesus and recognizing him when he speaks her name is hardly a proof for the primitive reality of divine love. Yet it is a clue, a suggestion, a provocation.

The Gospels frequently tell us that God is far better than we think. Often the parables of Jesus run to this conclusion. So the Prodigal Son becomes the occasion for insight into the more prodigal father. And the logic of a fortiori—if we, evil as we are, know how to give our children good things—makes it clear that God must be a generous, loving parent. If we ask God for bread, we will not get a stone. If we make God our treasure, we will not be disappointed: we will receive good measure, pressed down and overflowing. The workers hired at the eleventh hour receive a full day's wage because God is unthinkably generous. Jesus has called his followers not servants but friends, because God wants exchanges heart to heart. The passionate God uses our very weaknesses to break into our lives. We never escape the love of God. It stirs in our every yearning. Even when we grow cold, indifferent, and unfeeling, our inhumanity shouts that God is distressed. The Magdalene was a fitting apostle to the apostles because of what she was to announce and the mission her announcement was to found both were prodigies of love.

The Resurrection was a prodigy of love. God could not endure that that one in whom he was well pleased should remain in the prison of death. He had to liberate the liberator, freeing Jesus from the last enemy, the most implacable foe. Dying, he destroyed our death. Rising, he restored our life. So has faith long understood Jesus' being raised by the Father. The love of the Father for the Son could not suffer separation. By extension, the love of the Father for the friends of the Son, the members of his body, could not suffer their separation from their Lord. Mary Magdalene was as well poised to grasp this prodigy as a human being could be, because her love was so ardent. In fact, the physical return of Jesus to her simply sealed and ratified the identification of her self and cause with his, a relationship that had been growing for some time. He was the gist of her life. When he returned to her, it must have seemed too good to be untrue, too perfect to be anything but God's consummation.

Mary's going to the apostles with the news of the Resurrection involves several ironies, of course. The leaders have not seen and need to be informed by an ordinary member, a layperson. The leaders were not faithful to the end, and by being faithful, this layperson had outstripped them in rights. The Lord had favored a woman, continuing the maddening intimacy with women that had distinguished his rabbinate from the beginning. If there was a single virtue confronting the apostles, it was passionate, womanish love. If there was a single lesson implied for the future work of the apostles, it was the primacy of passionate love—that which took Jesus through death, that which reached into death and drew Jesus out, and that which made Jesus most moved by the Magdalene. Amusingly, and sadly, most of these ironies remain relevant today.

If the church believed its own doctrines enough to act on them, would it not make passionate love of God the central concern and so relegate other ethical, spiritual, and practical virtues to subordinate roles? Similarly, would it not be no respecter of persons and stations but seek first to honor the great lovers of God? At one point in biblical history pious Gentiles seeking the true God were known as God-fearers. After the Resurrection, God-fearing was sublated into God-loving. Indeed, for Johannine theology, perfect love casts out fear (1 John 4:18) For this reason women like Mary could stay by the cross. She was not bowled over by the Resurrection, did not faint away at the return of the dead.

The touch I like best in the resurrection scenario is Mary's recognizing Jesus when he speaks her name. This communication is in keeping with the style of the Good Shepherd, who calls his own sheep by name (John 10:3). Mary had a very distinct identity with Jesus. He said her fairly common name with accents so special she knew it had to be the Teacher addressing just her. Or perhaps we should think of the lover's tones—soft, intimate, and reassuring. There is no evidence that Jesus and Mary were physical lovers, and Christian instinct generally has shied away from such a thought. But clearly Jesus was the throb of Mary's heart, the lover of her soul. As much as the feminine voice in the Song of Songs, she languished at his absence, yearned for his presence. For the words he spoke were living water welling up in her heart, slaking her great thirst for love. The words he spoke were eternal life, something that could stand against everything tawdry, spoiled, headed for the grave. He was the bread of her life. He was the wine of her joy. When he was resurrected, the heavens opened. She felt that earth pointed beyond itself. She knew the embrace of the Holy Spirit, the divine love that made earth beautiful.

This picture will all seem emotional indulgence unless one takes seriously the Johannine witness to the Resurrection and Mary's part in it. Certainly this witness is symbolic, metaphorical, a conundrum to literal minds. But this quality makes it more, not less, real; it becomes more pregnant for minds that would ponder the paradoxes of life and death, for hearts sure that God is deathless in the measure that God is aboriginal love. Women who love a romance, or who appreciate the historical patterns of patient fidelity, or who mourn the vulnerability of their best emotions therefore should regard the Magdalene as a most pertinent symbol. Red hair flying, face shining with tears, she rushed off to give the best conceivable news: love had won, the beloved was alive and would always be.

Discussion Questions

1. Why was Mary Magdalene the apostle to the apostles?
2. How did Mary experience love to be stronger than death?
3. What does Mary suggest about religious passion and the nature of the biblical God?

Note

1. See Jane Dillenberger, "The Magdalene: Reflections on the Image of the Saint and Sinner in Christian Art," in *Women, Religion, and Social Change,* ed. Yvonne Yazbeck Haddad and Ellison Banks Findly (Albany: State University of New York Press, 1985), pp. 115–45; Margaret R. Miles, *Image as Insight* (Boston: Beacon, 1985), pp. 75–81; Elisabeth Schüssler-Fiorenza, *In Memory of Her* (New York: Crossroad, 1983), pp. 323–33; Raymond E. Brown, *The Community of the Beloved Disciple* (New York: Paulist, 1979), pp. 183–98; E. Ann Matter, "The Virgin Mary: A Goddess?" in *The Book of the Goddess,* ed. Carl Olsen (New York: Crossroad, 1983), pp. 80–96.

19

Acts 18:26

He began to speak boldly in the synagogue; but when Priscilla and Aquila heard him, they took him and expounded to him the way of God more accurately.

Acts is the second volume of Luke's historical theology, covering the period from the ascension of Jesus to the arrival of Paul in Rome. For Acts the great drama is the spread of the church to the Gentiles. The first twelve chapters feature the apostle Peter and describe early Christianity in Jerusalem, Judea, and Samaria. The last sixteen chapters feature the missionary journeys of the apostle Paul. Our text occurs early in Paul's third missionary journey. Paul has sailed for Syria with Priscilla and Aquila (18:18). Apparently these two, who were wife and husband, went on to Ephesus, where they met Apollos, a talented convert from Alexandria. Their action in correcting him suggests their own better acquaintance with Christian doctrine and perhaps also their status as authoritative teachers.

The fact that Priscilla (or Prisca) is mentioned before her husband, Aquila, may indicate that she had a higher social status. He was a leatherworker—not a prestigious job—and she may have provided the means for their extensive traveling. They appear to have been Jewish Christians, expelled from Rome by the edict of Claudius (49/50 C.E.) that banned Jews. Moving to Corinth, they met Paul and then finally settled in Ephesus. Priscilla was one of the most prominent women in the early church, perhaps functioning much like a bishop. Her activities and status remind us that early Christianity was organized around house churches (assemblies that met in homes, often those of wealthier people) and that women held significant leadership roles, sometimes working jointly with their husbands.[1] To say the least, the early church did not spread because it boasted a celibate, all-male clergy.

One of the problems with the preaching of Apollos was that he knew only the baptism of John the Baptist. In other words, the full Christian view of initiation into the church, which is prominent in Paul's theology, did not figure in his preaching. Priscilla and Aquila probably drew from their fuller understanding of the paschal mystery. The center of Pauline theology was the identification of Christ with the church and so the participation of Christians in Jesus' passover from sacrificial death to resurrected life. Apollos was persuasive in declaring that Jesus had fulfilled the promises associated with the Messiah. Priscilla and Aquila could fill out the significance of such messiahship, speaking of the baptism that took believers down into Christ's death (to sin) and up into Christ's divine life (grace). They could tell him of the eucharistic memorial of Christ passion, death, and resurrection that riveted the memory of Christ's members. I picture them doing this ministry enthusiastically, graciously, in an effort to make a good work even better.

Nowadays women do exercise some leadership in the Christian churches. Both as ordained officials and through their competence as theologians, catechists, liturgists, and the like, women are preaching the gospel, helping fashion ethical and doctrinal decisions, promoting social justice, working for peace, counseling broken families, and accomplishing dozens of other good works. Yet, as in Priscilla's day, female leadership remains subordinate to male leadership in most cases. As Priscilla was the exception in being mentioned before her husband, so today only a few women church leaders predominate in joint ministries. Our patriarchalism may not be so overt and pervasive as that of the first-century eastern Mediterranean, but it remains powerful. If Priscilla were in our midst, what might she be saying and doing?

I think she might be saying, first, that sex is irrelevant to depth of faith or wisdom about salvation history. As a good follower of Paul, she probably knew sentiments such as that of Gal. 3:28: in Christ there is neither male nor female. Certainly she realized that sexual qualities remain influential after baptism, but probably she would rate them as less significant than the new life revealed and offered in Christ. Paul had made so much of his conversion experience (Acts 9:1–22; 22:4–16; 26:9–18) that any Pauline Christian was bound to think of Christ as alive in the church. When Paul had been persecuting the church, he had been persecuting the risen Christ—that was the burden of the revelation that changed his life. For Priscilla, to be fully alive was to be united to Christ, and to die was to gain fuller union with Christ. Christ fully alive was the answer to all the great questions: meaning, healing, new creativity. Compared with such an answer, the issue of sex roles had to be considered secondary.

Did Priscilla herself accept a secondary status in the church, and would she counsel her present-day sisters to do the same? I doubt it. The authority Priscilla shows in dealing with Apollos suggests that she enjoyed high status in the Pauline community at Ephesus. Far from being a backbencher, she took the lead and set a talented, most likely strong-willed man straight. It does not matter whether she had a formal authorization to decide matters of doctrine. In the early church existential authority, charismatic power, usually was the deciding factor.[2] If she manifested wisdom about the Christian gospel and clearly spoke in the power of Christ's Spirit, she was likely to get a respectful hearing. I think she would challenge her present-day sisters to follow her lead, lamenting the ways that church structures tend to constrain women's gifts but arguing that no one finally can constrain the Holy Spirit.

In good Pauline fashion, she might remind us that Christ set us free for freedom—that we might enjoy the liberty of the children of God (see Gal. 5:1). Surely a primary aspect of such liberty is developing one's religious gifts and exercising them on the church's behalf. If the church does not appreciate such gifts or want such ministry, so much the worse for it. The member's job is to offer the charismata welling up within her. That it may take time and cost pain to have these charismata recognized seems the rule of the game. Paul himself certainly encountered troubles and had to dispute with Peter to Peter's face. On his model, leadership in the early church was tempestuous, because Corinthians and Galatians and authorities of the mother church in Jerusalem all had their own ideas.

It is finally most important that all who have ideas and ministerial gifts should keep offering them. A universal church without many different voices, colors, and points of view would not be the whole Christ. We have to hope that these different voices sing in harmony enough to praise God rather than recall Babel. We have to insist that minimally they include sopranos and altos, as well as tenors and basses. And we have to scoff at those who want sisters and mothers to pipe down because it so long has been a man's church and Jesus did not make any woman one of the Twelve. Only a self-serving mind would close church authority to women on the basis of such an argument. Only a mind ignorant of Priscilla, Catherine of Siena, Teresa of Avila, Georgia Harkness, Janice Grana, and hundreds of other gifted churchwomen would not blush to make it.

Last, I think Priscilla would counsel present-day women to

be free in their ministerial collaborations. Why not labor with a spouse for the spread of the church? Why get hung up over whose name comes first, who does what part of the job? The point is to preach the message, symbolize the life. The point is to show that bread broken and joy shared are quadrupled when spouses, lovers, and friends experience them together in faith. Apollos did not know the baptism of Christ. He had not been exposed to chrismation, the strengthening of the Spirit for ministerial work and witness. And perhaps he also did not know the depths of the Pauline nuptial symbolism: Christ married to the church, Christ giving all spouses the model and context for their mutually ministerial love. Priscilla and Aquila could tell him about all this theology because it was their life, their experience, their gift from God. Other early Christians—single, celibate, widowed, gay—could have told him other stories, revealed other implications of the union between Christ and the church. There were many different roles to play, many different gifts to offer, as Paul had kept trying to teach the Corinthians. But Priscilla must have felt then, and probably would expect her sisters to feel today, that being a female Christian was as good a gift as any other. Standing on it as her particular platform, she gave good witness. I hear her saying to us, "What has changed in your day? Why can you not speak up, travel, and correct inadequate doctrine just as I did? We have only one Master, only one Lord. If you have gifts in his Spirit, for God's sake use them!"[3]

Discussion Questions

1. What might Priscilla and Aquila have learned from being cast out of Rome?
2. How did the informal structures of early Christian church life favor strong women like Priscilla?

3. What witness were Priscilla and Aquila giving as a ministerial couple?

Notes

1. See Wayne A. Meeks, *The First Urban Christians* (New Haven, Conn.: Yale University Press, 1983).
2. See Edward Schillebeeckx, *The Church with a Human Face* (New York: Crossroad, 1985).
3. On the presence of others, and so of community, in the very desire that constitutes the self and spurs it to develop its gifts, see Sebastian Moore, *The Fire and the Rose Are One* (New York: Seabury, 1981).

20

1 Corinthians 11:3

But I want you to understand that the head of every man is Christ, the head of a woman is her husband, and the head of Christ is God.

A serviceable date for 1 Corinthians is 54 C.E. Paul founded a Christian community at Corinth probably in the period 50–51, and this letter may not have been the first he wrote to his converts after departing from them.[1] Our text occurs in the midst of Paul's reply to various questions the Corinthians had put to him (7:1). These have included matters pertaining to sex and marriage (7:1–40) and matters pertaining to food offered to idols (8:1–11:1) Turning to a discussion of public worship and spiritual gifts (11:2–14:40), Paul first commends the Corinthians for imitating him and keeping the traditions he gave them (11:2). Then he sets up a convoluted discussion of what head covering is fitting for worship by offering the triad we find in our text.

The head of every man [person] is Christ, in the sense that all Christians are members of Christ. He is the leading organ of the organism he makes with his followers and so may well be called the head. Perhaps Paul also means that Christ is the leader, the one with the best call on the loyalties, of every human being God has made, because all of creation occurred in the Logos and holds together in him (Col. 1:16–18). Christ Jesus then functions as the paradigm, the exemplary cause, of all human beings—the head or leading case of the humanity God would create through faith and grace.

The second sort of headship that comes to Paul's mind is that obtaining in the Hellenistic culture in which he lives, moves, and has his being. The culture was patriarchal and simply assumed that the senior male was the head of the entire extended family. Thus both Colossians (3:18–4:6) and Ephesians (6:1–9), expressing the Pauline school, have household codes—precepts for keeping order—reflecting the hierarchical relationships between husband and wife, parent and child, and master and slave that obtained in the typical Hellenistic family. The presence of these household codes and of such sentiments as those in our text is in tension with egalitarian tendencies of both Jesus and the early Christian communities.

Jesus organized a community distinctly more egalitarian and less hierarchical than those prevailing in the Jewish culture of his time, although he did not challenge Jewish patriarchalism directly or directly sponsor the equality of women for leadership in his community. Paul's own thought in Galatians dissolves hierarchical distinctions between Jews and Gentiles, masters and slaves, men and women, as we shall see in the next reflection. What we may find in the household codes is thus an accommodation to the prevailing Hellenistic mores, that Christian assemblies and families not seem to stand out or represent anarchic tendencies.

What we find in this second of the three headships mentioned in 1 Corinthians 11 is more mysterious, although the best explanation still is an unthinking acceptance of patriarchal dualism. As both a Jew and a cultured Hellenist, Paul had inherited a culture in which men unthinkingly assumed they were to lead and women were to follow. I find this a more satisfactory explanation than theories that posit something more profound, because on some of Paul's own theological grounds, women should be as entitled as men to assume the lead in marriage or community affairs. Witness the example of Priscilla.[2]

The third headship, that of God over Christ, is a hierarchy understandable in itself but subject to clarification from trinitarian theory. Certainly Jesus related to God as a son trying to obey a father. Certainly the eternal Son, or Logos, is begotten and thus dependent. But Jesus and the Father are also one, and that mutuality stamps all the trinitarian relationships. Indeed, in the perfect divine community the only distinctions are relational. In being, holiness, love, power, and the rest, the Father and Son are equal.

Nonetheless, even when we admit that Paul is simply subjecting the Corinthians to dualisms they would have found familiar and acceptable, we have to point out that the middle one, placing husband over wife as her head, is more noxious than the other two. For while headship can distort the relations between Christ and a disciple, and in my protocols would cede to the image of friendship and mutual ministry, certainly it is understandable that Christ should stand first and the disciples second. He is master, and they are pupils. He is the vine, and they are the branches. Similarly, that God should be the head of Christ is understandable, all the more so when one is speaking of the religion of the man Jesus, who certainly approached God as a creature, however trusting and intimate.

But making a husband his wife's head destroys the basis for both Christian marriage and full love between the sexes. It assumes that maleness inevitably carries rights to leadership, talents for leadership, and that femaleness means being a follower. Indeed, it can suggest that femaleness means being a second-class possessor of humanity, since an important part of humanity is the capacity for initiative and responsibility. None of this implication is logically necessitated by making the man the head, but the historical record shows that patriarchal cultures have not bothered overmuch about logic. They have been preoccupied with power, determined that men should have the official say. By sanctioning this position, making it part of Christian anthropology, Paul did women a great disservice. However unwittingly, he supported the misogynism of his time and made more difficult the discipleship of equals that Christian love could have sponsored.

That Paul was shaped by dubious assumptions in these matters is confirmed by what we find later in chapter 11. The context is still the question of whether women ought to pray with unveiled heads, but much deeper views surface: "For a man ought not to cover his head, since he is the image and glory of God; but woman is the glory of man. (For man was not made from woman, but woman from man. Neither was man created for woman, but woman for man)" (vv. 7–9). This is so simplistic a reading of Genesis 2 that one has to say that Paul had not thought very hard about the creation of man or woman. Did he really think the point was Eve's issuance from Adam's rib? Did he really accept the notion that woman existed only to be man's helpmate or companion? Did he think woman was not an image of God? Perhaps he did, but if so he had not explored the heterosexual relationship as deeply as he should have.

For no one who has met a person of the opposite sex comparable in talent, education, and the other shapers of what makes a human being impressive has not been invited to realize that maleness and femaleness are simply two intriguingly different yet like ways of being human. And no one with reflective instincts has not drawn from this experience the realization that most of our social roles are conventions, most of our dualisms or hierarchies can claim no ultimate foundation. If women can be as witty as men, as insightful (granted equal education), or as faithful, then women can be as good leaders, as good heads. If leadership demands muscles, a loud voice, an aggressive personality, then leadership is being superficially defined. Christians, of all people, ought to reject a leadership not correlated with love and service. The Pauline school later recognized this requirement (Eph. 5:25), but without drawing fully liberating conclusions.

If the example of Christ was one of self-sacrifice, then self-sacrificing might be the hallmark of Christian headship. Certainly the stereotype in patriarchal cultures has been that women are more gifted at self-spending, serving their husbands and children. And certainly the reality has been that women to our day have been culturally conditioned to think relationally, to prize caring, to resist hierarchical structures and favor egalitarian models geared to sharing. The lack of ego strength that many women lament is a painful legacy from the historical distortions of what power and headship ought to mean. Insofar as power and headship have been defined as suiting only men and requiring male biological equipment, they have deprived the race of much talent and caused women great suffering. Insofar as Paul proved a major influence in Christianity, feminists rightly hold him accountable for a significant amount of such suffering. As well, feminist theologians insist that his prejudice, if not misogynism, cannot be part of revelation. Otherwise, not just Paul but divinity itself would be sexist.

Discussion Questions

1. How useful for Christian spirituality are images of headship and dominion?

2. What is the two-edged sword in woman's being the "glory" of man?

3. How valid is it to separate culture and revelation in Paul's message?

Notes

1. See Victor Paul Furnish, "Corinthians, the First Letter of Paul to the," in *HBD*, pp. 185–87.

2. See Elisabeth Schüssler-Fiorenza, *In Memory of Her* (New York: Crossroad, 1983), pp. 251–84.

21

ॐ

Galatians 3:28

There is neither Jew nor Greek, there is neither slave nor free, there is neither male nor female; for you are all one in Christ Jesus.

Galatians, like 1 Corinthians (and unlike Colossians and Ephesians), is considered a work from Paul's own hand. It seems to have been written fairly early in his missionary career (between 49 and 55 C.E.), and although scholars do not know precisely where Galatia was located, they tend to associate the Galatians with the Indo-Europeans also known as Celts. In other words, they were Gentile Christians. In Galatians Paul is much interested in the relationship between the law (Torah) under which he had lived as a faithful Jew and the gospel he had accepted when he converted to Christianity. He is arguing for the superiority of the gospel in this section, describing the law as a custodian superseded by Christ. The verses immediately preceding our text are relevant, for they show the logic Paul has been developing. Christian existence is a new thing: "But now that faith has come, we are no longer under a custodian; for in Christ Jesus you are all sons [children] of God, through faith. For as many of you as were baptized into Christ have put on Christ" (Gal. 3:25–27). Our text therefore is an inference from baptism and Christian existence.

What is Paul saying? That baptism makes a new creature. Just as Paul views Christ as a second Adam, a new start for the entire human race, so he views baptism as a rebirth, through participation in the paschal mystery of Christ. The person baptized into Christ becomes a member of Christ, one who shares in Christ's corporate being. This baptism has the rhythm of Christ's own dying to sin and rebirth to divine life. It takes one into the divine life, which is both sinless and deathless. So Christ, or the Spirit given by Christ, is the principle of a new state of existence. What held prior to faith and baptism may no longer hold. The distinctions, qualifications, and conditionings of one's life may have been superseded, rendered outmoded. In particular, the distinctions that organized Hellenistic culture along the hierarchical lines we saw in the last reflection have fallen away. They are no longer relevant. The baptized are new beings, and all their social relations should be reconsidered in light of the equality they now share as children of the one God, members of the one Christ.

At other times the fall of the divisions between Jews and Gentiles and slaves and free people would be grist for our reflective mill. Here let us content ourselves with meditating on the dissolution of the divisions, the hierarchical rankings, that previously had obtained between males and females. As we have seen, both the Jewish and the Hellenistic streams of Paul's culture subordinated women to men. In both, women were the second sex; men were the heads and prime instances of humanity. Here Paul is saying that all such thinking is outmoded. Although he himself continued to indulge it in 1 Corinthians (perhaps Galatians was written after 1 Corinthians and represents progress on Paul's part), when he considered the paschal mystery it seemed clear to him that men had no superiority in Christ. All superiority belonged to the

Resurrected One. In their complete debt to him, men and women stood as full equals.

Few readers will be surprised to learn that my prejudice is that Gal. 3:28 represents the better Paul, the Paul more serviceable not just to women but to the church as a whole. For the church as a whole, as well as feminists, needs to hear that God, at least, is no supporter of the discriminations against women that have caused us so much suffering. God, at least, is no sexist. In Christ—whom the Synoptics contemplated bringing the Reign of God, the new era when things finally would be as they were meant to be, and whom John contemplated as having, through the Incarnation, made all of human existence sacramental—women could be as fully human as men. Since full humanity was not a question of physical strength or even cleverness according to worldly standards but rather a question of opening to God and making God the love of one's life, with the consequence that one tried to love one's neighbors as oneself, women now suffered no debilities. They could be as fully human as men because they could be as good lovers of God and neighbor as men, as good disciples of Christ.

Was Mary Magdalene not as good a Christian as Paul? Had she not predated him in allegiance to the Master and believed at a time when Christ's defeats made belief more difficult? Paul had been knocked from his horse, practically forced into faith. Mary had loved Jesus while wretched and in her sins because he had dealt with her face to face, treated her kindly, affirmed her personhood, given her something worthy of her passionate love. Certainly Paul has been the more honored Christian saint, but it would not be hard to make the case that Mary had been just as good a believer. Anyway, in Christ such competition is unseemly and does not matter. In Christ, as Paul saw surpassingly well, the point is to play one's allotted role, do one's allotted loving. God gives all increase. Neither Paul nor Mary could do more than plant and water. Side by side, as brother and sister in faith, they made the case that male and female are secondary if not entirely irrelevant considerations. Primary is the new life of the Lord. Primary is the initiative of the Lord. Everything is grace, so all human pretension, concern for rank, and sexual boasting is folly.

I wish the present-day Christian community thought as radically as Paul thinks in Gal. 3:28. If it did, there would be much less suffering among the ranks and much less reason to wonder whether the church leadership is not hypocritical. To be sure, there is a logical case for saying that the equality created in Christian baptism, the radical dissolution of religious ranks and hierarchies, can coexist with secular inequalities, ranks, and prejudicial customs. But this logical case comes to grief as soon as one considers how Jesus lived and what the gospel is about. The gospel is not a series of academic exercises, a bunch of riffs and scales to demonstrate the virtuosity of God, all the things that might be. The gospel is good news for flesh-and-blood people—Jews, Gentiles, slaves, freed, women, men languishing apart from the kingdom, suffering because sin continues to mottle their lives. So it makes no sense to separate Pauline radicalism from practical policies and programs. If Paul seriously believed what he said in Gal. 3:28, he should have treated women and men as complete equals when it came to assigning leadership roles in the church, thinking through the relations of Christian spouses, considering who was the image and glory of God. At the least I find him guilty of inconsistency. At the most I find him hypocritical. Probably the truth lies somewhere in the middle. Probably he had yet to assimilate the implications of his own deepest insights and did not see that they promised a new social order in which no group would be licensed to oppress another.

For of course oppression had been common among the three groups whose antagonisms are dissolved in Gal. 3:28. Jews had been puffing themselves up and continuing to consider Gentiles unclean, people of lesser fitness for dealings with God. Gentiles had had their own prejudices and prides, but in the early Christian communities the Jewish view had more power, so it was Jewish privileges that Paul was undercutting. The same with free people and slaves. One of the shames of Pauline theology is that it tolerated slavery and did not see the incompatibility of slavery and the newness that came with baptism. In Paul's defense one can say that social change of any significance takes time to reveal its necessity. Still, Jesus had given Paul and the rest of the church a striking example in opening his fellowship to "sinners," people on the outs with respectable Jews in his day. Equally, he had admitted women to intimacy and discipleship as few rabbis of his time could have conceived. On the other hand, he had had few dealings with Gentiles (the Canaanite woman of Matthew 15 is an instructive and feminist exception) and had mounted no program against slavery. So even Jesus could be considered to counsel moving slowly and concentrating first on the inner, spiritual freedoms that are the essence of liberation.

Eventually, however, it should have been clear, by the very principles of the Incarnation, that faith cannot tolerate a divorce, a disharmony, between the inner and the outer. Eventually it should have become clear that, if women were fully the equals of men in faith and Christian life, they had a claim on equal rights in the public, civil sphere. The shame of much Christianity is that secularists appreciated this implication long before it became a respectable position within the church. Today sexism in the church is such an affront, such a confession of stupidity and unconversion, that it makes great numbers of women deaf to the church's message. If the church is going to preach a Christ that the female half of the race can accept, it is going to have to put its own house in order, make constitutional for its own people and practices the radical sexual equality we find in Gal. 3:28.

Discussion Questions

1. Why does Paul consider baptism a new beginning?
2. How radically ought one to take the dissolution of such opposi-tions as Jew and Gentile, male and female?
3. Does the dissolution of male and female mean a Christian unisex and common bathrooms?

22

Ephesians 5:25

Husbands, love your wives, as Christ loved the
church and gave himself up for her, . . .

Most scholars consider Ephesians a work by disciples of
Paul, probably written during the decade 80–90 C.E. The
main reason for doubting that it came from Paul himself is that
it differs considerably from the style of such letters as Romans
and 1 Corinthians, where Paul's own authorship is all but
certain. The style of Ephesians is rather liturgical, as though
the Pauline communities had had another generation in which
to contemplate the implications for worship of the union between Christ and the church. As well, Ephesians assumes that
Gentiles may be admitted into the church, whereas in Paul's
missionary days that was a burning issue. Finally, Ephesians,
like Colossians, seems to reflect the church's settling into its
Hellenistic surroundings. Whereas Paul's thought was formed
by the expectation of Christ's quick return to consummate
history, Ephesians has no such expectation. Consequently,
Ephesians is more accepting of the status quo, the social
relations obtaining in Hellenistic society, including the hierarchical rankings expressed in the Hellenistic house codes.
The potentially radical cut of the Pauline insight into sexual

equality has been tamed, rendered wholly spiritual. Now men and women may be equals in Christ, but they are not to think that such equality translates into parity in the household, civil society, or even the administration of the church.

Our text is part of an extended lesson the author is reading out of the gratitude believers should have for their new, liberated existence. One inference he would have believers draw is that they must be willing to show one another docility and service: "Be subject to one another out of reverence for Christ" (5:21). This is an admirable sentiment, inasmuch as it implies mutual respect and mutual ministry. If it led to women's putting themselves out to help men, and men's equally putting themselves out to help women, few fair-minded people could criticize it. Alas, that is not what the author has in mind, for the next verses try to integrate mutual subjection and reverence with a sexual dualism: "Wives, be subject to your husbands, as to the Lord. For the husband is the head of the wife as Christ is the head of the church, his body, and is himself its Savior. As the church is subject to Christ, so let wives also be subject in everything to their husbands" (5:22–24). Let us ponder these verses.

First, wives are to be subject to their husbands, but no parallel line immediately comes along to balance this admonition and bid husbands be subject to their wives. If wives should consider husbands like Christ, their Lord, and willingly submit to their husbands' wishes, why should husbands not consider their wives like Christ, and show a similar willingness to submit to their wives' wishes? Is it because the maleness of Jesus renders the symbolism sexist, prejudiced against women's equal humanity from the start? Or is it because the customs of the times blinded the author to more liberated possibilities—for example, to considering "Christ" a new, resurrected form of humanity in which sexual hierarchies would be insignificant? Gal. 3:28 certainly suggests this latter possibility, and Galatians was written long before Ephesians. I am afraid the author of Ephesians was all too human, all too little penetrated by the radical vision of the new life in Christ, and so could not see beyond the sexist assumptions of the day.

Such assumptions are explicit in 5:23: the husband is head of the wife, as Christ is head of the church—a figure we saw when reflecting on 1 Corinthians 11:3. There the stimulus to thinking about headship seemed to come from a question about women's worshiping with their heads uncovered. Perhaps the author of Ephesians has picked up this figure of head without considering the original context in 1 Corinthians. At any rate, the parallelism is that the husband is to the wife as Christ is to the church—no formula for equality. For even when one sets the mutuality of love as a brake on dualism between Christ and the church, religious instinct is bound to give Christ all the priority. On the other hand, why should the husband have all the priority in a marriage? If God made humanity male and female, if the two are to cleave together and make one flesh, why should the husband be the headlike, Christlike, and therefore Godlike partner? The only reason seems to be the author's acceptance of the cultural standards of the day.

Something specifically Christian does indeed emerge in 5:25, our quoted text, but the preceding verse has removed all doubt about the author's male chauvinism: "As the church is subject to Christ, so let wives also be subject in everything to their husbands" (v. 24). This statement stands alone, with no counterbalance about how husbands should be subject to wives. Clearly, the mutuality possibly implied in 5:21, where Christians were to be subject to one another (without further specification), was not what the author had in mind. The Christians to be subject to other Christians now are shown to be wives. Perhaps children and slaves also are implied. What is not implied is the subjection of husbands to wives. The author of Ephesians has no image of Christ's coming not to be served but to serve, of Christ's girding his loins and washing his disciples' feet (John 13), that would make subjection or service fitting for men. The best he can do is bid husbands to love their wives as Christ loved the church, giving himself up for her, that he might sanctify and cleanse her.

This sentiment, to be sure, has liberating possibilities, although the image of cleansing, which seems designed to extend the parallel between husband and Christ into Christ's work of redemption, quickly casts these in doubt. But if we stay with the love of Christ urged on husbands, we certainly can agree that wives would be blessed to have husbands showing them the self-sacrificing concern Christ showed for his followers. If we wish, we can make such love tender, gentle, generous. We can make it strong, courageous, encouraging. We cannot, however, make it fully mutual. We cannot avoid the implication that men are closer to Christ than women are, that men are fuller images of the Image of God.

In 5:28, after elaborating the figure of Christ's washing the church and making her (a bride) without spot or wrinkle, the author adds that husbands should love their wives as their own bodies and that loving one's wife is loving oneself—a nice enough thought, and one that has liberating potential for Christian sexuality. But what remains missing is the reciprocity. Does the wife love herself in loving the husband? Is the husband like the wife's own body? How much does the author have Adam's rib in mind? Why do we never see the countercurrent, the flow from the wife to the husband? The most plausible answer is that the author simply does not think of wives or women as the equals of men. They do not stand on the same footing and cannot be involved in a two-way flow. And yet it is obvious that good sexual relations in particular and good marital relations in general entail reciprocity, complementarity, mutual give-and-take, even in patriarchal cultures. It is obvious that many women take responsibility, initiative, and power, even though the prevailing customs grant the lion's share of such things to men. So the author of

Ephesians finally comes into focus as someone who has not plumbed the marital relationship very deeply. Such limitation does not completely vitiate the potential of nuptial symbolism for Christ and the church, but it does greatly limit the insight and help this author's use of such symbolism yields.

At the risk of repeating the obvious, let me say in conclusion that I do not accept the dualistic view of the sexes and the marital relationship presented here and do not consider it binding on Christian spouses. Appealing to male chauvinists, clerical or lay, it may be. Perversely satisfying, certain "total women" may find it. But it so shortchanges feminine human nature and so limits the potential of marriage that I cannot think it God's revelation. It is just not true that men by nature are the heads of women, the leaders in households, the superior in the marital relationship, the one who should receive subjection but not give it. Such a judgment shortchanges both women and men. As well, it blinks facts that always existed but in our day have become more widely known: the irresponsibility of many men regarding women, marriage, children, and family life; the leadership that women abandoned by men or simply pushed by their own talents exert when it comes to raising children, running a home, furnishing the domestic income. Worse, this view renders tilted if not impossible the play, prayer, shared suffering, and shared joy that free men and women can experience. It is another temptation for men to become paternalistic, head patting, superior, condescending, and overbearing and for women to become wrongly meek, docile, helpless, foolish, irresponsible, childish, and weak. Does God want weak, simpering women? Does God think men by nature nobly made to be heads? I cannot believe she does, because I know she sees more than I see, and what I see makes such a view laughable.

Discussion Questions

1. How acceptable is a counsel to mutual subjection—mutual willingness to serve one another's good and follow one another's lead?

2. How did Christ love the church and give himself up for her?

3. Is the nuptial symbolism of Ephesians 5 flawed in its foundations, or might it be saved to illumine both marriage and ecclesiology?

23

1 Timothy 2:11–15

Let a woman learn in silence with all submissiveness. I permit no woman to teach or to have authority over men; she is to keep silent. For Adam was formed first, then Eve; and Adam was not deceived, but the woman was deceived and became a transgressor. Yet woman will be saved through bearing children, if she continues in faith and love and holiness, with modesty.

Our text for this reflection is longer than is ideal, but each verse has had sufficient influence throughout Western history to merit consideration. The majority of scholars think the Pastorals (1 and 2 Timothy, Titus) came not from the hand of Paul but from members of the Pauline school writing early in the second century C.E. Apparently the church in our author's area was facing various disciplinary difficulties, and the author (presumably a male) felt free to write in Paul's name (such a practice of pseudonymous authorship was acceptable at the time) and give the remedies Paul might have prescribed.[1] For our purposes, the thing to note is the further hardening of the prejudices against female nature that another generation's worth of church existence had wrought.

In the section immediately preceding our text the author

has been concerned with good order at prayer. Men are to pray lifting their hands and not quarreling. Women are to adorn themselves modestly and avoid costly ornamentation (perhaps a hint that the author thinks attractive women might distract men from prayer). The adornment of women the author approves is moral: good deeds. This advice certainly could be unobjectionable, but it also could be the view of a puritan, a moralist in the pejorative sense.

Our verses move from moralism to outright discrimination. First, a woman is to learn in silence, submissively. In other words, she is always to consider herself a pupil and comport herself docilely. Even if her male teachers are spouting nonsense? Even if they give no grounds for intellectual respect, credibility, or granting them the existential authority that only wisdom merits? Apparently so. A woman is a beginner, a person always to be in tutorship. Why so? The author postpones saying, letting us first think the answer is obvious, a matter of common sense. Perhaps it was in his Hellenistic circle, but even when Hellenistic women had little teaching authority, they were not automatically silent. The author is making things quite convenient for himself. He is dictating rather than reasoning, vetoing dissent rather than giving explanations and inviting discussion.

Verse 12 spells out the tactics that Paul supposedly would cite to justify this imposition of silence on women: it is unacceptable for women to teach or have authority over men. Does that mean Priscilla overstepped Christian boundaries in correcting Apollos? Should Mary Magdalene have stopped her mouth and not explained to the apostles about the resurrected Christ? Or has the pseudo-Paul so gotten his wind up that biblical memory and Christian common sense have deserted him? Is he so frail in ego that the word of a weak woman might shatter his churchy authority? I see no good explanation for his stance. It seems all too like the bullying to which dictators everywhere resort, especially when their case is weak. It is all too reminiscent of John 3:20: "For every one who does evil hates the light, and does not come to the light, lest his deeds should be exposed." If church officials have decent, holy policies, why need they fear the reactions or speech of any believers, women or men?

In verse 13, we get the mythology that is standing duty for a rationale. First, women are to be quiet because they are the second sex. Adam was formed first, so men are the heads, the ones with power, the sex commissioned to name the animals and order the world. Woman is a tagalong, formed from an expendable rib, acceptable mainly because otherwise man would be lonely, would have no one to applaud at the Big Game. Second, women are to be quiet because their prototype fell, initiating the disaster of human alienation from God (original sin). To the mythology of creation has been added the mythology of the primal disobedience. The Yahwist is being manipulated to ends he or she never foresaw. Just as this pseudo-Paul forgets the delight the Yahwist has Adam find in Eve, so he forgets the free agency of Adam in taking the fruit and disobeying the divine command.

Foolish as it is to try to dissect myths, one must meet pseudo-Paul on his own ground and point out that, even according to the logic of the patriarchal Yahwist, he is inconsistent. Either Adam is sovereign and responsible for everything noble in human nature, or he is equal to Eve in human frailty. One cannot have it both ways. If he was made first and thereby constituted the teacher, with Eve ever after to be the pupil, why did he not take charge in the matter of the fruit and nobly render the Lord full obedience? What sort of professor one day tells his students to keep quiet and listen, because he has all wisdom, and the next day not only foolishly follows the student's false step but abdicates all responsibility for doing so? Only a sorry professor, a very unmanly teacher. On both counts—both claiming all authority and pushing blame off on the student—the teacher, like the emperor he would like to be, has no clothes. His claims stand revealed as naked foolishness. So too in the ecclesiastical life.

Last, in verse 15 we hear the author's remedy for fallen womankind, the way the dumb, transgressing Eve is to justify God's having made her. If she bears children, Adam may be able to put up with her. If she shows faith, love, holiness, and modesty, God may escape being charged with a great mistake. How generous of our author! Nobility is again obliging by recognizing a few facts: we obey the command to increase, multiply, and fill the earth only with the help of women; holiness in either sex automatically commands respect. But of course this last verse was as hurtful to women as the prior three. For it confirmed the patriarchal prejudice that most of a woman's value resided in her body—indeed, in her sex organs—and it slanted women's religion in the direction of false modesty: keeping covered, rocking no boats, saying "Yes, m'Lord" day and (more important) night.

I have no quarrel with faith, love, holiness, and even modesty, of course. Each admits of an acceptable—indeed, an admirable—denotation. And I feel no need to disparage motherhood, the docility without which one cannot learn, or the silence befitting those who in fact are beginners or in fact here and now do not know very much. In the proper context, and granted parallel evaluations of male faith, love, holiness, modesty, and docility, none of the virtues here assigned to women need be prejudicial. Similarly, granted a parallel view of men's contributions to the survival of the race, responsible fatherhood definitely included, I think that to love women's procreative capacity and the feminine virtues it has encouraged throughout history (care, nurturance, sympathy, support) is a sign of Christian insight. But the prejudicial, if not outrightly vicious, interpretation of Yahwist mythology we find in this text triggers my bile. How arrogant and self-serving! What a dangerous precedent, as generations of patriarchal Christian leadership have proved! Pseudo-Paul has on his head guilt for a significant amount of the violence and humiliation women have suffered throughout the Christian era. Among the biblical wrongdoers, he stands out as a paramount oppressor.

At the end of the preface to the new edition of his book on religion and violence, Robert McAfee Brown quotes St. Augustine concerning hope. The quotation and Brown's gloss would be moving on most any occasion, but they strike me as especially powerful when we think of the violence women have suffered. Indeed, Brown's preface explicitly focuses on the rise of feminist consciousness in the fifteen years since the first edition of his book, and I suspect that the text from Augustine worked in his subconscious in part because it speaks of two daughters. If Pseudo-Paul, the author of 1 Timothy 2, were in my confessional, I might well assign him as penance long meditations on Augustine-in-Brown.

> How is this hope [of Latin Americans for liberation] to be made a reality? That is the subject for another book. But the basic outlines of the direction were given by St. Augustine, a millennium and a half ago. "Hope," he said, "has two beautiful daughters, anger and courage; anger at the way things are, and courage to work to make things other than they are." We need to enlist hope's daughters in the current struggle, as sources of power, being assured that when anger and courage are present the final word is not despair, not quiescence, but hope. We have learned that from our third world friends; we have seen it in their faces and in their lives and deaths. Let us hope, in turn, that some of it may rub off on us.[2]

Amen!

Discussion Questions

1. How likely are wise teachers to tell their students to keep silent?

2. Why does the author of 1 Timothy 2 employ the Yahwist mythology of Genesis 2 and 3?

3. How should feminists employ the two daughters of Augustinian hope in the church today?

Notes

1. See James L. Price, "Timothy, the First and Second Letters of Paul to, and Titus, the Letter of Paul to," in *HBD*, p. 1075.

2. Robert McAfee Brown, *Religion and Violence*, 2d ed. (Philadelphia: Westminster, 1987), p. xxii.

24

Revelation 12:1

And a great portent appeared in heaven, a woman clothed with the sun, with the moon under her feet, and on her head a crown of twelve stars.

The Book of Revelation is a specimen of the literary genre known as apocalyptic. This genre flourished in Judaism from the third century B.C.E. (1 Enoch) to the end of the first century C.E. (4 Ezra, 2 Baruch). The second half of the Book of Daniel is apocalyptic, occasioned by the abominations committed by Antiochus IV Epiphanes in 168 B.C.E. The New Testament Book of Revelation therefore follows in a well-established tradition. Like its predecessors, it presents itself as a heavenly disclosure of what God is soon to do on behalf of God's suffering people. Whether Revelation was occasioned by the persecutions inflicted on Christians by the Roman emperor Domitian in 95–96 C.E. or represents more general frustrations of believers who had expected their faith to usher in the Parousia or bring them worldly success, it has merited its place in the Christian scriptural canon because of its brilliant imagery for the divinity of Christ and the struggle between evil and God's grace.

Revelation is a highly structured work, most of its sections being formed by sevens: letters (2:1–3:22), seals (6:1–8:1), trumpets (8:2–11:19), and so on. Our text comes at the beginning of a section (12:1–15:4) presenting seven unnumbered visions.[1] This imagery has served the Catholic liturgy for the feast of the Assumption of the Virgin Mary into heaven (August 15). On its own terms, it seems more concerned with portraying the church as the mother of all believers being threatened by Satan, the personification of evil: "She was with child and she cried out in her pangs of birth, in anguish for delivery. And another portent appeared in heaven; behold, a great red dragon, with seven heads and ten horns, and seven diadems upon his heads" (12:2–3). The eschatological, final period of salvation history has come, causing the warfare between God and Satan to intensify. The woman (the church, or perhaps the mother of the Messiah) is being pursued by diabolical evil, which senses that its end is near.

A woman clothed with the sun shines with heavenly light. In putting the moon under her feet, the author may be subjugating the pagan mysteries, or simply giving her as a pedestal the lesser light of the firmament. The twelve stars of her crown may represent the twelve tribes of Israel, symbol of the fullness of God's first people. Insofar as the woman is a daughter of Israel, she reminds us of the function of Mary, mother of the Messiah, as well as the provenance of the church, born among the Jews. Revelation throughout consciously draws on imagery of the Hebrew Bible, the thought-world on which it depends. And even when it is powered by Christian convictions about a new dispensation, it remains indebted to the prophets for prior glimpses of what the heavenly life of God, the Ancient of Days, might be like.

I am interested in the imagery of our text as a final tribute to the potential of biblical woman. From her comes godly life, which an incarnational faith cannot separate from physical birth, education, and culture. I fully agree that this godly life also comes from biblical men. My feminism is not a plea for separatism, let alone an argument for the superiority of women. But here I want to reflect on the legacy that biblical women have passed down, usually anonymously, through a faith that got little public recognition or applause. Here I want to applaud the female quotient of the suffering, faith, and love that have kept the heavens open as a realm of hope and beauty generation after generation.

The odd thing is that even detractors of women, even those who resonate to Pseudo-Paul and want women to stay in the back benches with tape on their mouths, regularly go teary about the faith of their mothers, or their grade-school teachers, or their washerwomen, or their wives that occasionally showed them the real proportions of the life God everywhere is in labor to bring forth. As many commentators on the images of women in various societies have pointed out, regularly women are both lauded and despised all out of proportion to what men (who are considered normal, prescriptive humanity) receive. Regularly women are both goddesses and whores. They stand either on a pedestal or in the gutter. Authorities consider them more virtuous than men (because less warlike and physically destructive) and less trustworthy (because more emotional). So they become the salt of the earth, but they are not to teach in church. We revere them as the source of life and faith, but they remain daughters of Eve, the primary transgressor.

What we seldom do is take women as coconstitutive of humanity with men. Therefore we seldom go out of our way to incorporate women's views, instincts about faith, or advice (even about family life) into our law and policy, civil or ecclesiastical. Pseudo-Paul and his ilk have done their work well. Women have been not only the second sex but the silent sex, the deviant other to whom it would be dangerous to give 50 percent of the votes, offices, money, and responsibility.

And yet women, biblical and nonbiblical, inevitably have claimed 50 percent of the grace of God and 50 percent of the

religious return to God. Stereotypically through their influence on children, but in fact in dozens of other ways, women
have spoken the words of eternal life enabled by Jesus: you are
not alone. All will be well. I love you. Do not be so hard on
yourself. Your pain is my pain. Stay, abide, endure—the
morning will bring light.

Many spiritual writers assume that, in its relations with
God (whom they can consider only male), the soul is feminine. Because women are the sex considered patient, second-
ing, receptive, and attentive, while men are considered ac-
tive, initiating, and controlling, the soul waiting on the divine
initiative, being cleansed by the action of the Spirit, "naturally" seems feminine. Future spirituality may well question
all of these assumptions and produce some interesting varia-
tions stimulated by portraying the divinity in feminine terms.
But for the present the soul, the religious personality, remains
stereotypically feminine. This characterization is not all bad,
however, because it can help us appreciate the primacy of
patience, in the root sense of suffering.

Because we are ignorant, mortal, sinful beings, we spend
most of our lives trying to outlearn or outgrow an ego-
centricity that simply does not fit the facts of either the
universe or the ways of God. The universe pays an individual
creature little heed, being primarily concerned with such
transpersonal tasks as oscillating atomic fragments and explod-
ing huge stars. The ways of God are kindly, loving, and wise,
so they cannot indulge our childish assumption that we are
the hub of the universe. God has to wean us from this sweet
but unhealthy pap. We have to learn, usually through mis-
takes and pains, that the most significant things about us
invite awe, worship, and waiting for God's revelation.

Behind us are the eons of creation and the primordial
silence and power from which they issued. Before us is the
darkness of the future, the great unknown guarded by death.
We may imagine the future with figures like those of John of

Patmos, loving the possibility of the 144,000 who sing before the divine throne all the while. We may hope to attend the nuptials of the Lamb, so worthy because he was slain for us and our salvation. But we have no vision of these things, only faith.

So we wait, reflect, and act as best we can for the good of the earth, the loosening of our neighbors' bonds, and we pray for enough light, or enough congeniality in the darkness, to bring us to whatever resolution of these mysteries God has in store. We learn to love and cling to the yes, the amen, that God has said to us in Christ, God has spoken through the prophets, God has poured forth in our hearts through the Holy Spirit. These so slender, apparently fragile supports have to see us through. Often we wonder how they will ever bear the weight of our torpor, our misgivings, our inability to pray and believe. But, like the pale green bamboo of a Zen garden, they prove resilient, able to bend yet bear, able to resurrect regularly in beautiful new strength.

Or they prove to be like small, quiet, unobtrusive, even neglected women: the heart of the gathering, the emotional center of the family, the daily provider of food and comfort. If God is real and God's love is serious, what happens each day as we eat, drink, earn a living, guide the kids, make love, hurt one another, grow weary, worry, take a deep breath, praise the stars, and lay ourselves down to sleep praying God our souls to keep must be the marrow of salvation history. The woman clothed with the sun must illumine the dusty, blinking sisters who have not had time to look out the window or who would not feel the splendors of the spiritual life had much reference to them. The Bible tells us only indirectly about the average woman's lot. It only hints at the faith that has seen most mothers and lovers through. But occasionally a woman emerges clothed with symbolic power, and the light she casts makes it credible that everywhere God is using the patience and wisdom of women to build up what is wanting to the sufferings of Christ and fill out the complement of the kingdom. Now and then, I look around and think I see such symbolic women on all sides.

Discussion Questions

1. How does the church mother religious life, and what is she now in labor to bring forth?
2. What changes in spirituality might come if theologians were to promote the femininity of God?
3. How has female patience served throughout salvation history?

Note

1. See John Carmody, Denise Lardner Carmody, and Gregory A. Robbins, *Exploring the New Testament* (Englewood Cliffs, N.J.: Prentice-Hall, 1986), pp. 310–11.

Conclusion

We have seen twenty-four snapshots of biblical woman—hardly a full portrait, but perhaps enough to suggest important features. What ought we to take away with us? What are the motifs most worth pondering?

The main benefit I have derived from biblical studies in recent years has been a better appreciation of the complexity, diversity, and richness of faith and God's dealings with human beings. The Hebrew Bible is such a marvelous collection of overlapping, contradictory, alternative traditions and visions that one willing to read it through and hear its own voices is bound to come away marveling at the humanity of revelation. The patriarchs and matriarchs are flawed, conniving, yet admirable human beings. When Sarah laughs (Gen. 18:12), we are bound to sympathize: much in the effort of human beings to accept the bounty of God is ridiculous, a divine comedy. David is despicable in his dealings with Bathsheba and Tamar, yet a part of his soul remains attuned to God, wants to be better. The wife of Job has the smallest of parts, yet trying to imagine her share in Job's sufferings adds a whole new dimension to the story.

So too with the New Testament, where the briefer scope seems only to intensify the claims and implications. The widow of Nain (Luke 7) is pathetic precisely because she has lost a son who was her defense against total vulnerability. From such panicky need as hers, faith can issue? Apparently so, and thereby an interesting lesson. The mother of the sons of Zebedee (Matthew 20), aggressively seeking their promotion, is equally human, although less perceptive about the nature of the Messiah. Still, we meet her at the cross, persevering to the end, learning in full sorrow what Jesus' messiahship entailed. As with Peter and Paul, the women of the New Testament must slowly learn what faith in Jesus implies. They are not saints hatched in a day. So much the better for us.

If Scripture is a privileged lens onto the divine nature, a place where God has partially removed the veil around God's creative love and given us stories true enough to satisfy our souls, the women and men we meet in the scriptural pages are more consoling than daunting. For while a few of them do extraordinary things, most of them muddle through, coming to the finish line with many scars and bruises. If they are admirable, it is because when they fall they get up. When they sin and miss the mark, they repent, confess their sin, and start walking again. *Homo viator* is one good name for this biblical humanity: people on pilgrimage. *Femina viator*, many of the sisters we have contemplated could be called. Few of the biblical paradigms we have studied saw God directly, spoke with the divinity face to face. All shared our condition of darkness, confusion, and doubt. Even those privileged to encounter the Lord—Eve, the women who were friendly with Jesus—felt they were in over their heads. What was going on was too rich, too mysterious, for them to comprehend. They could only shake their heads and try not to pass out from dizziness.

In another context I would make the point that these biblical women have their equivalents in the nonbiblical cultures and scriptures. With admittedly different theological and cultural overtones, Hindu, Buddhist, Chinese, Japanese, Muslim, and other religious women have begged to be taken from the shadows and images into the divine light. If their petitions have been answered, usually it has only been for a brief hour. That hour might sustain them ever after, but back in the confusions of daily life they too would soon be.

God has not made us angels. Strangely, we find so obvious a truth hard to appropriate. The less we are centered in God, able to call the divine mystery the most real thing in our lives, the more we feel guilty for not having clarity in our minds and hearts. We think our work, family life, friendship, and prayer are confused, complicated, shot through with gray compromise because we lack the moral fiber, the discipline, and the goodness to make them tidy. It takes us years and much suffering to let ourselves suspect or hope that God lives on the near side of our human messiness and that God can be found long before we reach the border of tidiness and clarity. Biblical faith, rightly expounded, could have eased our learning process. The saints of both Testaments, and Jesus himself, urge in virtually every story that we look at what is before our eyes, get in touch with what is beating in our hearts, realize that God is as near as life's mystery.

Before our eyes are such wonders as biological life—in trees changing in the autumn, in babies crawling toward trouble, in old people bent yet smiling, in lovers lost in a world of their own, in pups, chipmunks, blood given at a Red Cross center, tears shed at a funeral, and cheerleaders kicking high for a touchdown. These things are absolutely ordinary yet utterly miraculous: how did they get where they are? How do they work as they do? What do their beauty and pathos mean? Where are they going, and how are they influencing us?

The same wonder attaches to the sufferings we find so commonplace, so regular a feature of our newspapers and newscasts that we are bound to feel groggy, punchy, unable to take in so much pain, so much horror. If the people in our neighborhood and at our place of work do not suffer gross physical ills, they suffer emotional and family problems. If our town is not suffering bombs or floods, it is suffering crime or unemployment or child abuse. All of this grief—near and far, domestic and foreign—also is mysterious, cause for wonder. We cannot understand it. Sometimes we think we cannot bear it. But we know, in that silence of our hearts we too seldom visit, that any real "God" has to be involved with it. We know that faith must be the substance of the things we hope will happen to alleviate such suffering, to give it some border and meaning.

The faith of biblical women and men reposed in God's

covenants. The pledges of the One who had led the people out of Egypt, inspired Moses to proclaim the law, enabled the exiles in Babylon to hang on, rescued the Mordecais and Esthers of the postexilic period, and shone from the face of Jesus of Nazareth did not remove the sufferings of daily life or eviscerate the beauties, but they did render both bearable, sufficiently possibly meaningful, to make human life seem good. Because of the covenants, it both mattered and did not matter whether one prospered or declined, lived or failed to live a saintly life, experienced pain or knew joy, came to the end full in years or died in the flower of youth. As married to human time, pledged to human beings, incarnate as our brother, divinity let all events matter exceedingly. Not a hair of people's heads was insignificant. If God so clothed the grass of the fields, how much more did God care about and care for human beings, us of little faith. If God had led the people out of Egypt with a mighty arm and had given his only Son for the world's healing, how could God fail to give us of little faith all God had to give? Nothing could separate us from the love of God—because of what God was, who God had shown divinity to be.

Nothing was inconsequential. Yet, equally, nothing was divinity itself. Always the infinite qualitative distinction between Creator and creature obtained, counseling against idolatry. The trick therefore was to catch the Creator in the creature. The trick was to look daily life full in the face and glimpse a smile, sometimes wan, that implied more than daily life on its own could warrant. All people die. Biblical women knew this fact as well as did their pagan forebears and successors. Yet they were privileged to wonder whether union with the deathless God did not shift the meanings of that elementary proposition. Did all people in fact die if God had promised the Davidic line an unending partnership? Was Israel perhaps granted a share in the divine vitality, a promise that its offspring, numerous as the stars in the heavens or the grains of sand along the seashore, would always be, as long as human beings drew breath?

And what about death after Christ? In the twinkling of an eye, at the sound of a trumpet, everything might be changed. Mary Magdalene knew: her master, who had been laid in a tomb, called her name. Martha and Mary knew: if the master had been there, Lazarus would not have died, and when the master came, Lazarus was called forth from the dead. What was going on? How could "death" and "life" become so symbolic, so slippery? No one understood, but many suspected it had to do with letting God increase and human presumption, assumption, despair, arrogance, and the rest yield center stage. On center stage ought to be the primordial mystery, the bedrock yearning, the wonder the world stirred up whenever one gave it a chance and shifted from being busy to being attentive and contemplative.

God contemplated becomes God redefining what is real, realigning people's priorities. The first thing is to be, to live, to share in the divine grant of creativity. The first thing is to find a way to say yes back to the yes echoing in one's being, calling in one's loins. Biblical womanhood is formed by this responding yes. Though it seem slain by patriarchal abuse, yet would it trust that God was no patriarch, that God had purposes patriarchy never knew. Though it suffer calumny, yet would it continue to raise its voice in protest, continue to sing praise to a Lord it did find authoritative. Our religion is ourselves at these bedrock, daily, incarnate tasks. Our womanhood or manhood is our sexed suffering of God's primacy and mystery, sometimes to the point of a felt share in God's resurrecting love. If we can say yes through the pain, we can shelter in biblical religion. If we can admire people who told God what was on their minds and in their hearts, we can think biblical woman a part of ourselves wanting to get out and take over.

Discussion Questions

1. How does a covenantal relationship with God make daily life both more important and less important?

2. How does a covenantal relationship with God make women free to be themselves?

3. Where does the yes of faith come from, and through what does it move?

Appendix
Twenty-Four Further Texts
on Biblical Woman

The Bible offers almost limitless resources for reflection on the religious lives of women. I would find it easy to write reflections on each of the texts listed below, using the same general format I have employed for the reflections in this book. In each case it would be useful to set the historical and literary context. Then one would be free to muse about the implications the text bears nowadays, following the train of images and feelings that had been aroused. As religious, the reflection ought never to wander far from the divine mystery—God's presence as the indefinable origin and goal of our knowing and loving. As feminist, it ought always to seek the illumination that comes when women are considered strict equals with men in the possession of humanity.

These additional texts, like those we have previously considered, show women suffering the prejudices of patriarchal culture. On the other hand, they also can provoke a better appreciation of how biblical women coped and how God was not a patriarch but a real divinity dealing with women as cherished individuals. Finally, I might note that most of the benefit these texts can provide comes from discussing them in a circle. It is as stimuli to free-flowing exchanges of people's experiences, ideas, hopes, and pains that they will be most liberating. My best wishes to all who take them up.

Further Texts from the Hebrew Bible

1. Genesis 16:6

2. Genesis 24:67
3. Genesis 25:28
4. Exodus 20:12
5. Leviticus 18:20
6. Deuteronomy 24:5
7. Judges 14:17
8. 2 Samuel 6:16
9. Job 2:9
10. Proverbs 6:25
11. Song of Songs 3:1
12. Isaiah 49:15

Further Texts from the New Testament

1. Luke 7:13
2. Matthew 20:21
3. Acts 16:16
4. Revelation 17:1
5. Mark 10:11
6. Matthew 5:27
7. Luke 13:12
8. Matthew 15:28
9. John 2:4
10. James 1:27
11. 1 Corinthians 7:14
12. Galatians 4:30

Bibliography

The following works offer a beginning in the two areas this book has joined: biblical studies and studies in women's liberation. The works marked with an asterisk straddle the two areas and might with equal justice have been placed with works concerning biblical topics.

Biblical Studies

Achtemeier, Paul J., ed. *Harper's Bible Dictionary (HBD)*. San Francisco: Harper & Row, 1985. An up-to-date reference work produced by members of the Society for Biblical Literature.

Brown, Raymond, E. *The Community of the Beloved Disciple*. New York: Paulist, 1979. A stimulating study of the forces behind Johannine Christianity.

Carmody, John; Carmody, Denise Lardner; and Cohn, Robert L. *Exploring the Hebrew Bible*. Englewood Cliffs, N.J.: Prentice-Hall, 1988. An introductory college text, focusing on literary interpretation and present day significance.

Carmody, John; Carmody, Denise Lardner; and Robbins, Gregory A. *Exploring the New Testament*. Englewood Cliffs, N.J.: Prentice-Hall, 1986. An introductory college text, focusing on literary interpretation and present day significance.

Childs, Brevard S. *Introduction to the Old Testament as Scripture*. Philadelphia: Fortress, 1979. A survey of the recent scholarly literature, with special concern for the final, canonical editing.

Gottwald, Norman K. *The Hebrew Bible: A Socio-Literary Introduction*. Philadelphia: Fortress, 1985. A masterful overview with special interest in the sociological forces at the origins of the different strands of the Hebrew Bible.

Knight, Douglas A., and Tucker, Gene M., eds. *The Hebrew Bible and Its Modern Interpreters*. Philadelphia: Fortress, 1985.

Reports on the state of research in the different subspecialties of Old Testament studies.

Levenson, Jon. *Sinai and Zion*. Minneapolis: Winston/Seabury, 1985. A stimulating essay in Old Testament theology, focusing on the two poles of law and cult.

Meeks, Wayne A. *The First Urban Christians*. New Haven, Conn.: Yale University Press, 1983. A sociological approach to Pauline Christianity.

Plaut, W. Gunter, ed. *The Torah: A Modern Commentary*. New York: Union of American Hebrew Congregations, 1981. The text, a translation, and a full commentary (citing both recent and classical [talmudic] sources) on the first five books of the Hebrew Bible.

Schüssler-Fiorenza, Elisabeth. *In Memory of Her*. New York: Crossroad, 1983. The most significant work on the status of women in early Christianity and a pioneer effort in feminist biblical hermeneutics.

Terrien, Samuel. *The Elusive Presence*. New York: Harper & Row, 1978. A full-scale biblical theology, encompassing both Testaments and stressing the reality of the divine mystery.

———. *Till the Heart Sings*. Philadelphia: Fortress, 1985. A study of the biblical views of manhood and womanhood that stresses the liberating possibilities.

Trible, Phyllis. *God and the Rhetoric of Sexuality*. Philadelphia: Fortress, 1978. A pioneer work that explores the positive aspects of women's experience in the Old Testament period.

———. *Texts of Terror*. Philadelphia: Fortress, 1984. A troubling book that concentrates on some of the worst instances of the abuse of women during the Old Testament period.

Witherington, Ben, III. *Women in the Ministry of Jesus*. Cambridge: Cambridge University Press, 1984. A close textual study of New Testament sources for Jesus' treatment of women.

Studies in Women's Liberation

Atkinson, Clarissa W., Buchanan, Constance H. and Miles Margaret R., eds., *Immaculate and Powerful*. Boston: Beacon, 1985.

Feminist studies in women's historical roles and images in a variety of cultural settings.

Brown, Robert McAfee. *Saying Yes and Saying No*. Philadelphia: Westminster, 1986. Case studies in the tension between allegiance to God and allegiance to Caesar.

Bynum, Carolyn Walker. *Jesus as Mother*. Berkeley: University of California Press, 1982. Studies in the feminization of Jesus in medieval piety.

Carmody, Denise Lardner. *Seizing the Apple*. New York: Crossroad, 1984. A feminist spirituality of personal growth.

———. *Women and World Religion*. 2d ed., rev. and exp. Englewood Cliffs, N.J.: Prentice-Hall, 1988. A complete redoing of a brief survey of data from the world religions, originally published in 1979.

*Carmody, John. *Like an Ever-Flowing Stream*. Nashville: The Upper Room, 1987. Meditations on peace and justice, based on texts from the Old Testament.

———. *The Quiet Imperative*. Nashville: The Upper Room, 1986. Meditations on peace and justice, some based on texts from the New Testament.

Coles, Robert, and Coles, Jane Hallowell. *Women of Crisis*. 2 vols. New York: Delta/ Seymour Lawrence, 1978, 1981. Moving interviews with women caught in difficult circumstances who have exhibited great faith.

Conn, Joann Wolski, ed., *Women's Spirituality*. New York: Paulist, 1986. Essays in the history and present requirements of women's religious development.

Dinnerstein, Dorothy. *The Mermaid and the Minotaur*. New York: Harper & Row, 1976. A powerful, psychoanalytically oriented study of the effects of women's being the predominant childrearers.

Eck, Diana L., and Jain, Devaki, eds. *Speaking of Faith*. Philadelphia: New Society Publishers, 1987. Short, readable reports on women's religious experience around the contemporary world.

Falk, Nancy A., and Gross, Rita M., eds. *Unspoken Worlds*. San Francisco: Harper & Row, 1980. Studies of women's religious experience in various non-Western societies.

Gilligan, Carol. *In a Different Voice*. Cambridge, Mass.: Harvard

University Press, 1982. A stimulating study of women's personality development that stresses women's orientation to care and relationships.

*Gutierrez, Gustavo. *On Job*. Maryknoll, N.Y.: Orbis, 1987. A quite scholarly study of Job, with special interest in Job's identification with the poor and in the detachment genuine religion inculcates.

Haddad, Yvonne Y., and Findly, Ellison B., eds. *Women, Religion, and Social Change*. Albany: State University of New York Press, 1985. Studies of the religious factors in women's social evolution in a variety of cultural settings.

Haughton, Rosemary. *The Passionate God*. New York: Paulist, 1981. A brilliant extended essay on how God works redemption through human weakness.

Lerner, Gerda. *The Creation of Patriarchy*. New York: Oxford University Press, 1986. An innovative, scholarly study of the origins of male dominance in ancient Near Eastern civilization.

Miles, Margaret R. *Image as Insight*. Boston: Beacon, 1985. Studies in the historical influence and significance of religious imagery that often illumine the lives of women.

Moore, Sebastian. *Let This Mind Be in You*. Minneapolis: Winston/Seabury, 1985. A powerful theological reflection on the pains and possibilities of selfhood.

Olsen, Carl, ed. *The Book of the Goddess*. New York: Crossroad, 1983. Cross-cultural studies in female divinity.

Rosaldo, Michelle Z., and Lamphere, Louise, eds. *Woman, Culture, and Society*. Stanford, Calif.: Stanford University Press, 1974. Anthropological studies of women's roles and status in a variety of cultural settings.

Ruether, Rosemary. *Sexism and God-Talk*. Boston: Beacon, 1983. One of the most thorough feminist constructive theologies.

Warner, Marina. *Alone of All Her Sex: The Myth and Cult of the Virgin Mary*. New York: Knopf, 1976. A historical study of Mary's images and quasi-divine influence.